DEFINE AND DELIVER EXCEPTIONAL CUSTOMER SERVICE

DR. KELLY HENRY

Published by Advantage Publishing Group

Copyright ©2020, Kelly Henry

ISBN: 978-1-7349756-9-7   Hardcover
ISBN: 978-1-954024-00-7   Paperback
ISBN: 978-1-954024-01-4   Ebook

https://drkellyhenry.com/
To contact, please e-mail: drkel@drkellyhenry.com

SPECIAL INVITATION

Thank you for picking up my book. My goal is to serve and help business owners ignite passion and enthusiasm for exceptional customer service. I believe this book will lead you to your goals.

I want to invite you to join me for a free call. Working together with clients, I see businesses make incredible advances, and I'd love to see how I can help you.

Schedule your free call with this link.

https://drkellyhenry.as.me/

TABLE OF CONTENTS

"

I've learned that people will forget what you said, people will forget what you did, but people will never forget how you made them feel.

MAYA ANGELOU

INTRODUCTION

It is common knowledge that small businesses have a difficult time sustaining and succeeding over a long period.

According to Fundera.com, 20% of small businesses fail within their first year, 30% fail by their second year, and 50% fail after 5 years in business. The kicker is 70% of small businesses fail in their 10th year in business. That's a lot of hopes and dreams crushed and flushed down the drain. Many small businesses do survive and remain for many years, but never generate the success that the owner had dreamed and worked for.

Why is it that small businesses have such a difficult time surviving and thriving?

There are many reasons for this. According to Fortune.com, the most common reason for small business failure is there's no market need for the product or service provided. If that's the case, then you're screwed. Either you come up with a product or service that's needed, or you fail. The next three most common reasons for small business failure are the business ran out of cash, they didn't have the right team, and they were outcompeted. What do these 3 reasons have in common? They are all directly related to customer service. Customer service has a huge influence on sales and cash flow. Customer service directly affects the attitude and actions of the team running the business. Customer service directly affects a business's competitive advantage.

This is not a book about customer service; this is a book about success!

This is about how to run and sustain a successful business. This book is not just for the businesses that are struggling and are on the brink of closing. This book is also for the successful businesses that are doing well but could be doing even better. This book is for one-person operations or businesses with thousands of employees. It is for the brick and mortar businesses and online digital businesses. It doesn't matter the business type because the principles on how you treat customers are the same for every business.

My goal in this book is to help businesses to go from surviving to thriving and from thriving to dominating. This is accomplished through creating and enhancing customer service and developing a service culture and attitude within the business.

I know this because I've lived it for over twenty years.

I've used the ideas and principles in this book to build and run three very successful businesses. I've seen these principles transform the businesses of my clients, helping them grow and creating greater success. I didn't write this book on what I've heard about; I wrote this book based on first-hand knowledge and experiencing the incredible benefits of creating a service culture-based business.

Every business owner believes their business provides great customer service, and this is partially true. Most businesses do have a few pieces and aspects of great customer service in play. The problem is the owner doesn't realize the pieces of bad service that creates a negative effect that causes a huge loss of customers and significant profits (I will go into much more detail about this later in the book).

What's important to remember is there is absolutely no downside to improving a business's level of customer service. There's a laundry list of benefits, but the three that generally make the greatest impact are retaining more customers, creating more new customers and business and finally, significantly increasing profits. What business doesn't want those three benefits to happen regularly?

You might be thinking this all sounds great, but can improving your customer service really make that big of an impact on a business? This is not just my point of view and personal experience. Consider successful businesses such as Amazon, Southwest Airlines, Zappos, Apple and Chick-fil-A have all been built on the foundation of exceptional customer service.

What do you have to lose by reading this book? Nothing! My promise to you as you read this book is, you'll find simple strategies, ideas and principles. If you take action and implement them, you'll notice and see significant change not only in your business success but also the atmosphere of the business itself. It'll be a happier, friendlier and better place to work.

Don't wait to read this book, and as you read, don't wait to act and implement the information you learn. If you know what to do and don't do it, it's as bad as not knowing the information at all. Don't wait until it's the right time to implement because it will never be the right time. Don't worry about being perfect; only think about doing and figure the rest out as you go. As our 33rd President, Harry S. Truman, said – "Imperfect action is better than perfect inaction."

Read and take action now; I promise you won't regret it.

PART ONE:
DEFINE IT

66

Don't mistake movement for achievement. It's easy to get faked out by being busy. The question is: busy doing what?

JIM ROHN

CHAPTER 1:
CUSTOMER SERVICE DEFINED

There's a story about a person who dies and meets St. Peter at the Pearly Gates. Peter tells this person that God is running a special! They can test out both Heaven and Hell for a day and then pick which one they want to spend eternity in. So, the person gives Heaven a try first – and it's really great. It's just as expected. The next day this person goes to Hell. They are transported to a beautiful beach with clear blue water and plenty of sunshine. They have a personal cabana and all the food they can eat. It ends up being a perfect day of fun in the sun. When they return to the Pearly Gates, Peter asks which place would they like to spend eternity? The person decides to go to Hell – they had so much fun on the beach! So, they are transported again to the depths. But this time, there is no beach, sunshine, clear blue water, or fun. There's only fire and brimstone, sulfur and pain, screaming and the gnashing of teeth. Soon Satan comes to greet the person who asks what happened to the beach, the water and all the fun from yesterday? Satan replies, "Yesterday, you were a prospect, today you are a client."

Customer service isn't sales. Businesses will often spend thousands of dollars to attract new customers, and not a single dime to keep the ones they've got.

I liked to think of my office as a customer service clinic that happened to also do chiropractic care. Our number-one priority was to make the patient feel their best not only physically, but psychologically every time they set foot in the building. The goal of every business should be to make every customer feel valued, important, liked, and special with every interaction, with every employee, on every day. The number-one reason a customer will leave a business is that they feel unappreciated.

A good place to start a book about customer service is to define precisely what it means:

cus·tom·er serv·ice

noun
exceptional customer service is when a business makes the customer feel their best during the time they spend with it

This is accomplished through the actions and attitudes of the business. I'm not talking about a customer service department or a system set up to help customers if they have a question or a problem about a product or service. I'm talking about a philosophy and culture which is at the very core of the business.

A customer service culture permeates throughout every aspect of the business from the top down and everything between, extending throughout the relationship of the customer. Many businesses will attempt to excel at customer service when trying to make a sale but are terrible after the customer makes a purchase. Unlike the story about heaven and hell, a business needs to be even better with their service after the sale.

After buying an office from a retiring chiropractor, my family and I moved to a small town in New Mexico. It became quickly apparent that customer service was lacking for many of the businesses in town. There were often no greetings, no smiles, or eye contact. We felt like we were an inconvenience trying to do business with some of these companies. It didn't take me very long to decide that my office would not treat my patients that way. My clinics would excel at great customer service and make our patients feel important and valued. This started my twenty-year journey of studying, utilizing, improving and coaching exceptional customer service skills, and leading me to write this book.

Unfortunately, my experience with those businesses in New Mexico, is very common among many businesses across the United States. According to the DiJulius Group, roughly 80% of businesses across the US at best perform average to very poor levels of customer service. This means the top 20% performing above average service are reaping phenomenal benefits from doing so.

It doesn't take a whole lot of energy to give great customer service! Appreciating a customer takes just as much energy as ignoring them. It all boils down to the attitude and the culture of the business. Either the business is completely committed to great customer service or it's not. Some businesses understand this and gain the tremendous rewards of committing to exceptional service. Others ignore the concept of great service and wonder why the business doesn't grow or is just barely surviving no matter what else is done to make it grow.

Now you have a working definition of what great customer service is. In this book, we'll identify the specific actions and attitudes that help to create a customer service culture that can bring great success for you and your business.

"

Remember, people will judge you by your actions, not your intentions.

ANONYMOUS

CHAPTER 2:
HOW CUSTOMER SERVICE HELPS YOUR BUSINESS

How Can Improved Customer Service Help Your Business?

When I talk about how important great customer service is, business owners often agree with me. They know it would be a good idea. Some tell me their business already offers great customer service. Some tell me it would cost too much or take too much effort to overhaul their current systems.

I want to clarify some of the incredible benefits that are achieved when a business dedicates itself to the mindset, attitude and culture of providing exceptional customer service. The information I'm about to share isn't entirely new information but make no mistake – this information is not outdated. These benefits are as true today as they were fifty years ago. Some of the mechanics and actions may have changed over time, but the benefits remain the same. These benefits hold true for any business in any industry, whether it's a brick-and-mortar business or a strictly online business. The reason these benefits are achievable no matter the business is because it's all about how you treat people.

The majority of customers want to be treated with respect. When a business offers this consistently, customers realize that there's something different about the business. This makes the customer want more of that feeling and to tell others about what they've experienced. This creates the loyalty that stimulates incredible growth for a business. It's no coincidence that many of the biggest and most profitable companies in existence today were started on the foundation of providing exceptional customer service.

Important benefits of delivering exceptional service:

1. Increased new customers
2. Increased retention and repeat business
3. Increased profits and income
4. Happier business environment
5. Distinct competitive advantage

These are phenomenal benefits that make a huge difference in the success of every business. Let's dive in and take a little closer look at each benefit.

INCREASED NEW CUSTOMERS

The purpose of a business is to get a customer, keep a customer and make a profit. What I've found with many businesses is they don't exactly line up with that purpose. They work very hard to get a customer and to make a profit but do virtually nothing to keep that customer. Many businesses spend a lot of money on marketing and advertising to attract new customers. Obviously, this is important because new customers are the lifeblood of these businesses. If a business misses the mark on working to keep customers and is only focused on getting customers, they generally have a difficult time growing and even sustaining the business. The objective of a business should be to *make customers who make customers.* This happens when a business becomes fantastic at delivering exceptional customer service. They cause their customers to become advertising agents. They are the mouthpiece for the business.

When customers feel valued and important, they want others to experience those same feelings, so they become excited to refer others. We all know that the best kind of new customer is a referred one. This is why exceptional customer service is called the new advertising. The last ten years I was in practice, roughly 90% of my new patients were referred to my office. I did very little external marketing because I didn't have to! When you create raving, loyal customers that help your business thrive, you don't have to rely on advertising to help you survive.

INCREASED RETENTION AND REPEAT BUSINESS

The central focus of improving customer service is to increase customer retention. Let me repeat that: it is all about customer retention. The purpose of a business is to get a customer, *keep a customer*, and make a profit. I've talked to so many business owners that only concentrate on getting customers in the door to make a profit. This is a stressful way to run a business because you're in constant need of new customers to make ends meet. It's a hamster wheel of advertising, chasing leads, making sales, dealing with complaints, losing the customer and having to hunt for more new customers to make up for the ones you just lost. It is much more expensive to acquire a new customer than to keep an old one. Yet many businesses will never recognize and change the things that cause them to lose their customers. They only focus on tactics to bring the new customer in the door to make enough profit for that month. I cannot stress enough the importance of focusing on retaining customers, which directly correlates to incredible growth and profits for the business. Providing exceptional customer service dramatically increases retention, which leads to increased referrals, which leads to dramatically increased profits and income.

MORE PROFITS AND INCOME

Who doesn't want to make more money? Increased profits are the byproduct of the first two benefits I just described. When a business increases the retention rate of their customers, which increases the number of referrals into the business, you will make more sales, which equates to more profits. The focus of exceptional customer service should be on creating relationships and making every customer feel great. When this is done consistently, increased profits will naturally follow.

HAPPIER BUSINESS ENVIRONMENT

One of my first jobs was mowing commercial properties for a landscaping company. This wasn't a particularly difficult job. We were a crew of four and we mowed a few properties a day. We started at 7 am and were off at 3:30 pm, which left my afternoons open to work for my own mowing business. The worst part of working for that landscaping company was getting chewed out constantly by the crew leader, the manager, or if you were really lucky – the owner. I learned very quickly what to do and what not to do, but I focused primarily on not drawing attention to myself and avoiding the wrath of my superiors. I basically worked in fear that summer. One morning near the start of working with the company, the manager waved down the truck I was in as we were leaving for the job site and chewed me up one side and then down the other. He bellowed that I should get my rear in gear or be fired. I did, in fact, get my rear in gear and right out of that job. This was a terrible work environment and one I struggled to get up and head to every day. Maybe you've had a similar work experience in a toxic work environment? These situations lend to absolutely no one being happy, especially the customers, who have a front-row seat to the misery of mistreated employees. Many businesses use fear and intimidation tactics with their employees. The main problem with that (and there are several problems) is that employees will treat the customers very similar to how they are treated as employees. It's naive to think that you can treat employees terribly and expect them to put on a smile and give great customer service.

To create a culture of exceptional customer service, you must treat the employees as well or even better than the customers. The employees must feel appreciated to make customers feel appreciated. When employees are treated with respect it transforms the work environment. Employees enjoy coming to work, doing their job. They enjoy and take pride in taking care of customers. They tend not to complain, and they want to do well because they know they will be recognized for it. They get along with other employees better and they want to stay with the company because of the fun and fulfilment they are having. It's the difference between having to work and wanting to work.

Treat the employees well, and the atmosphere in your business will be of community, team, support and happiness. This creates a positive reinforcement loop. The employees are treated great and they treat the customers great. When the customers are treated great, they compliment and praise the employees, which causes the cycle to go on. You can't go wrong promoting happiness and a team mentality in your business.

DISTINCT COMPETITIVE ADVANTAGE

Every business is trying to get an advantage over the competition. Whether it's the product, the location, technology, or the price there's always some angle to exploit over the competition. The most common advantage default is price. The problem with seeking your competitive edge with pricing is that you can only drop or discount it so much before it takes out too much of your profit margin.

If a business places its sole advantage on the price, it becomes very difficult, if not impossible, to create loyal customers that continue to buy because this type of customer only wants the best price or lowest offer. If one business doesn't have the lowest price that day, then the customer moves on to the business that does. Without a meaningful connection, it is very difficult to build a following. Tinkering with your price points lowers profit margin, creates continual marketing needs, and results in a high volume of customers coming in and a high volume of customers going out.

An infinitely better competitive advantage is to focus on the service provided. Developing and improving exceptional customer service distinguishes a business and brands them in a different way. Surveys show that when a customer does business with a company that gives great service they are willing to pay around a 17% premium because of that great service (American Express 2017 Customer Service Barometer). This is the exact opposite of trying to be competitive with pricing. The customer is happily willing to pay the premium because of how they are treated by the company that provides great service.

Now, charging a premium is not the objective of providing exceptional service, I'm not advocating price-gouging your customers. The customer who is consistently made to feel valued, however, won't mind paying a little extra for service that goes above and beyond. They will enthusiastically tell those they know about their experience with the business and highly recommend it. Making the customer feel their best when they are with you becomes a huge competitive advantage for your business!

How does exceptional customer service help your business?

- Increased new customers
- Increased retention and repeat buying of existing customers

- Increased profits and income
- Happier business environment
- Distinct competitive advantage

66

**Nobody counts the number of ads you run;
they just remember the impression you
make.**

WILLIAM BERNBACH

CHAPTER 3:
THE 5% BUMP

Marketing is the price a business pays for poor customer service.

I'm not against marketing. It's an important part of building a business, especially when starting out. Problems occur when an established business becomes solely focused on marketing for new customers and doesn't develop a system to keep those customers. I was guilty of this in my clinic for many years. I enjoyed and valued the new patients a great deal. I wasn't focusing on the established patients as much as I should have. Once I figured out the value of nurturing relationships with established patients, my practice exploded in growth and profit. And when I made that switch, I stopped virtually all of my outside marketing because 90% of my new patients came in as referrals.

What exactly is the "5% Bump"? It's a statistic that shows that increasing customer retention by just 5% can increase profits between 25% and 95% (Bain and Company). If you're like me, you're thinking it seems too good to be true. So, let me explain how this is possible.

When a business is committed to providing exceptional customer service and developing a customer service culture, one benefit is increased customer retention. As more customers enjoy the great service and continue to buy, they also refer others to experience what the company offers. When you increase the retention of customers and new customers are being referred into the business, it will drive up profits. As new customers are consistently being referred into the business, the need for marketing is decreased. The money being spent on marketing can be saved, which increases the bottom line. When you retain more customers, they refer more customers, which drives up profits. It is really that simple.

Always remember that customers will focus on the service they received much longer than the price they paid. When the service is based on making the customer feel great, they remember that and will want more. When the service is based on making a transaction and not on great service, the customer will more than likely leave. Fifty-one percent of customers will never do business again with a company after one bad experience. Companies based in the United States lose from $62 to $80 billion a year in lost sales because of poor customer service. If your business is not focused on exceptional customer service, these two statistics should scare you. Running an established business based on marketing and price is like paddling upstream with a wooden spoon: it can be done, but it is very difficult. Focusing on improving customer service and retaining customers is like paddling downstream with an oar. It's a whole lot easier and a lot more fun.

The 5% Bump should never be the goal, it is simply the outcome achieved from the great service provided. Developing a great customer-centered culture doesn't automatically and immediately retain every customer. It doesn't address all other business problems. It does, however, create the right climate. Customers will experience fewer problems. A business with plenty of customers and plenty of profits is a happier company.

Here's one final point about the 5% Bump. It's not that difficult to achieve. It doesn't take a massive overhaul to establish an improved customer service system in your business. It only takes commitment to do the little things that make a huge difference in a very consistent manner. The little things create major results, and we'll look at these small actions in the following sections.

PART TWO:
UNDERSTAND IT

"

Change the way you look at things and the things you look at change.

WAYNE DYER

CHAPTER 4:
CUSTOMER SERVICE FOUNDATIONS

Have you ever built a house or a building? The first and most important thing is to lay a firm and solid foundation. Developing and implementing the strategies for exceptional customer service does not differ from constructing a building. You have to lay the proper foundation to build upon to make it as effective as possible. Many businesses claim to have great customer service strategies that improve their customer service. The problem is they have no foundation in place. Just like a house being built without a strong foundation, problems arise because things were not *established* correctly. Customer service shouldn't be a pet project. It isn't the flavor of the month or a new shiny object discarded after a few weeks. A customer service culture should be a guiding principle and one of the most important aspects of every business. I thought of my clinics as a 'customer service clinic' that just happens to do chiropractic work. Many of the most successful businesses in the world share the same philosophy.

As we go through these foundational principles and you understand them, you need to look at them as guardrails for the decisions you make about your customer service. You can also think of them as the filters you must look through in making decisions that will affect your customer service.

PRINCIPLE #1 – CUSTOMER PERCEPTION IS EVERYTHING!

Have you ever been to a movie with someone, and after it's over, you rehash it and break it down together and talk about what you liked or didn't like? Often, you'll find you have differing opinions. You liked it and they didn't. You liked this part and they hated that part of the movie. You love this actor and they don't see the appeal. There's no right or wrong to opinions. It's just preference based on your perceptions and experiences. The same holds true for your customers. Their perception of your business is based on their reality and their life experiences.

It doesn't matter what you as the owner thinks is good customer service. It doesn't matter what your spouse, employees, friends, family members or anyone else think about your level of customer service. If the customer doesn't perceive it as exceptional, then it isn't great customer service. Again, customer perception is everything! There's a business study that reported some interesting findings (Bain and Company). They discovered that 80% of surveyed business owners believed that their business performed superior customer service. When the consumers of these same businesses were surveyed, only 8% of the consumers reported these companies gave superior service. That is a 72% gap between what the owner and the consumer thinks! Who's right? According to Principle #1, the customer is right, because customer perception is everything. It's a big problem if business owners believe their company already provides superior customer service and doesn't see the need to improve it. This delusion can be very costly over time. Don't let that be you and your business. You have to base your customer service on the perception of the customer and not the opinion of anyone else – even your own.

PRINCIPLE #2 – CUSTOMER PERCEPTION IS DRIVEN BY HOW YOU MAKE THEM FEEL

How do customers want to feel? They want to feel appreciated, valued, welcomed, special, and important. Briefly - they want to feel like a rockstar. The vast majority of your customers want to feel appreciated. I would venture to guess you want the same thing. Every aspect of your business should focus on making the customer feel valued and important. Keeping that mission in mind will move a business a long way towards offering great customer experiences. This will involve communicating with the customer to know if they are feeling valued. Checking in with them regularly helps to eliminate the owner and customer perception gap. In my office, our mantra was: "Treat the Customer Like Royalty and You Will Gain Their Loyalty."

PRINCIPLE #3 – CONSISTENCY

One of the guiding philosophies for my life and businesses is that consistency is the key to success. Regardless of what I'm trying to achieve, it takes consistency in both thought and effort to accomplish it. This is incredibly true as it relates to customer service. It's very confusing and frustrating for a customer to experience inconsistent customer service. Whether it's from one day to the next, or one employee to the next. Ultimately, inconsistent customer service is no better than average or poor customer service because the customer will only remember the poor service. The good experience will be forgotten. Remember: it takes twelve positive experiences to make up for one bad experience!

You must first commit to making customer service part of the fabric of your business and then consistently implement and train to constantly improve it. Half-hearted commitment will frustrate your customers, your employees and yourself. If you frustrate your customers enough – they won't be your customers for long. That's how incredibly important consistent relationships are. Now, I'm not saying you and your employees must be perfect all of the time. Perfection is unrealistic. Later in the book, I'll discuss exactly how to handle situations when you and your employees make mistakes. Customers recognize the difference between a one-time screw-up and a lack of consistency in your service.

Every principle, rule and action I've outlined in this book can be implemented. If they are performed correctly, but not done consistently with every customer and with every interaction, on an everyday basis, you will only create problems and will never be able to achieve the reputation for providing exceptional customer care.

Remember these Three Foundational Principles:

- Customer Perception is Everything
- Customer Perception is Driven by How You Make Them Feel
- Consistency is Key

"

The successful person has the habit of
doing the things failures don't like to do.

THOMAS EDISON

CHAPTER 5:
RULES TO PLAY BY

I've just described the foundation principles of exceptional customer service and how vital they are to developing a successful customer service culture. Now I want to look at the rules to guide these concepts and specify the actions that need to be taken.

Building a customer service culture is like learning to play a sport. First, you generally have to learn the principles and objectives of the sport. Then you learn the rules of the game and finally, you learn the actions to play the sport correctly. If you don't know the principles or rules and just go out and play the sport, you could assume you're playing the game right, but in reality, there's no structure and it will result in chaos. Chaos in customer service means losing customers and losing money.

Here are my Three Platinum Rules for Exceptional Customer Service to help you play your best game.

RULE #1 – DEVELOP AND MAINTAIN A SERVICE MINDSET

The very essence of customer service is to **serve** the customer. Many businesses *say* they want to serve their customers, but their actions speak differently. The customer gets the we're-here-for-you lip service, that ultimately becomes we're-here-for-you-sometimes and really only-if-it's-convenient-for-our-business. Your service attitude should be an unrelenting focus on taking care of the customer. It shouldn't matter what's going on in the business or with the employees, the focus of your company should always be on serving the customer.

Always remember that the business is there for the customer and not the other way around. The customer always comes first and should always be treated that way. Think of it like this: Your business is a dog and the customer is your owner. The dog is always way more excited to see the owner than the owner is to see the dog. Look first to serve and make your customers' lives better.

"You can have everything in life you want if you help enough others get what they want."

Zig Ziglar

It takes many people to run a successful business, from the owner to executives, managers, staff, employees, etc... You have to always remember that if you don't have customers, you don't have a business! If you don't have a business, no one else in the business matters. When you remember how valuable a customer is, it's not that hard to focus on serving them.

The service mindset was a philosophy in my offices; however, a few times, my focus on serving each and every patient would stray. This never caused me to harm a patient, but my focus was divided between the patient and something else I had a concern about. When employee issues, family issues, a business problem, or a personal conflict took over, the critical numbers for my practice would decline. Collections, patient visits, and new patient numbers would go down along with office and employee morale. It didn't take long to realize what was happening and correct the situation. As soon as we were refocused, my practice numbers would bounce back. What you think about is what you bring about. Never take lightly or underestimate the tremendous importance of developing and maintaining a relentless focus of always serving the customer first.

RULE #2 – FOCUS ON BUILDING RELATIONSHIPS – NOT ON MAKING TRANSACTIONS

Building relationships with customers is a vital component of creating loyal customers. The greatest customer-centered companies are fantastic at this.

People do business with those they know, like and trust. When a business develops and builds relationships, they're creating bonds that are very difficult to break. That's why it's so difficult to move from one state or city to the next. You have to break the bonds with all the clients and businesses you know, like and trust and then try to establish new relationships with new businesses. That can be very challenging and take a lot of time to do. When my family moved to Texas after living in New Mexico for twenty years, it took us six months to find a church that was right for us and a year and a half for me to find a barber I liked.

There's a very simple way to help build relationships with your customers. All it requires is to become interested in the customer by asking questions. Your questions should be specific. You could ask about their family, their career, their hobbies and what they do for fun or about their history and what brought them to a particular city or place. The key is to get the customer to talk about themselves. In general, people love to talk about themselves, and if they feel like you are genuinely trying to get to know them, they open up to you. When you get them to open up you, the walls break down and you create bonds.

In the initial stages of getting to know a new customer, you often get information that will help you understand how you may best serve them or identify the best product to fill their needs. As a chiropractor with a new patient, I would ask about hobbies or occupation. This would help me to get to know the person, but it also gave me insight into what might help or hinder their recovery.

Don't let your customer leave your business without finding out something about them. Keep notes about what you learned so you can follow up with them about it with subsequent interactions. This leaves an incredibly positive impression on the customer, and they'll feel you consider them more than just a transaction to your business. My employees and I did this regularly with our patients. I would ask follow-up questions based on our last conversation, which would often impress the patients. All it took was asking the right questions and recording it to make a lasting impression. The bottom line is when you focus on building the relationships and not just making money, you are reinforcing the service mindset and building up a loyal following of customers.

RULE #3 – STRIVE TO BE THE BEST PART OF THE CUSTOMER'S DAY

In my office, this is more than a rule. This has become a part of our mission statement. I highly encourage you as a business owner, executive or leader to seriously consider adopting it into your company as your service mission statement.

Our goal was to do two things: be the best part of the patient's day, and to have everyone who came to the office leave feeling better than when they arrived. There were countless times that a patient would thank my staff and me for making their day better. We couldn't change the circumstances of their day, but they left the office feeling better about themselves and this impacts their ability to handle the day ahead of them. We strived to be the bright spot for them.

When a customer comes to your business, it's important to be aware that they're probably dealing with some kind of problem or issue. The customer may be stressed, upset, tired, scared, nervous, sick, or unhappy. The key is not to judge them because of the state they are in. Your job is to empathize with them, and serve them, and do everything you can to make them feel important.

When your business consistently strives to be the best part of every customer's day it can be an absolute game-changer. Because customers rarely experience this kind of treatment anywhere else in their lives. Once the customer has experienced this kind of treatment, they'll want to experience more of it and tell others about it, too. It's human nature to gravitate to those who value us and make us feel special. This is true in all of our relationships, and it certainly holds true for business relationships. No matter how good or bad, happy or sad a customer presents themselves to your business, focus on being the best part of their day. A service mindset, with unwavering focus on the customer, and contributing positively to their day, will bring about incredible results and experiences.

Remember these Three Platinum Rules of Exceptional Customer Service:

- Develop and maintain the service mindset
- Build relationships – not just focusing on making transactions
- Strive to be the best part of the customer's day

66

Everything in the world we want to do or get done, we must do with and through people.

EARL NIGHTINGALE

CHAPTER 6:
LOYALTY VS. SATISFACTION

I have never heard of a company that strives to irritate, be indifferent or claim they could not care less about the customer (although I've done business with a few that sure act like they do). No one sets out with the slogan: "We care about our customers until they try to do business with us." Creating customer satisfaction is almost always the intention.

> sat·is·fac·tion
>
> noun
> fulfillment of one's wishes, expectations, or needs, or the pleasure derived from this.

How does a customer feel satisfied? Let's say you head to the store for some items. You run in and the items are stocked, you head to the checkout and there's a lane with no waiting. You check out easily, leave, and head home. By definition, you were satisfied. The store fulfilled your expectations and needs. The problem is that satisfaction leaves no lasting impression. It basically leaves customers in a neutral position. They are indifferent. If something goes wrong with an interaction, or the customer gets offended or upset, then obviously they will feel negatively toward the business. If a business exceeds the customers' expectations and "wows" them, the customer feels positive and has the incentive to be loyal to the business.

Granted, a satisfied customer is much better than an irritated customer, but in reality, neither will show much *loyalty* to the business. The upset customer won't be loyal because they're ticked off and the satisfied customer won't be loyal because nothing happened. Creating a loyal customer is the golden ticket.

Customer satisfaction equates to mediocre or average customer service. Creating customer satisfaction is basically one small step up from customer dissatisfaction. Mediocre customer service is such a common occurrence that for most customers, it feels like the norm. If they experience terrible service, they rarely complain (even though it's easier than ever through social media). Generally, they'll accept it and find a competitor that only has average service which is at least a step up. Sometimes, they'll come across a business that gives superior service – the kind of service that didn't just meet expectations but went above and beyond to the point of amazing the customer. This kind of experience for the customer is so different and so unusual that it leaves an incredible impression on them. This is where the magic of customer loyalty is created.

loy·al·ty
noun

1 the quality of being loyal.
2 a strong feeling of support or allegiance.

You want to create allegiance in your customers. You want them to support you and be completely dedicated to your business. Sports fans support their team – win or lose. The fan is on the side of that team. In essence, you want a bunch of fans of your company.

Creating loyalty with your customers is virtually guaranteeing your future business success. Creating a satisfied customer only takes care of a single transaction. One customer will be dedicated and the other will be indifferent. Which would you rather have for a customer? One that stays with you or one that's off to your competitor because they got a coupon in the mail? A satisfied customer will shop anywhere. A loyal customer will fight before they leave a business. When a business is focused on creating a loyal following of customers, they keep a loyal following of customers.

So how do you create loyalty?

Businesses seem to understand that creating a loyal following of customers and improving customer service is important. They might think that it's difficult to do and would require too much effort and expense. Fortunately, that is not the case. Providing exceptional customer service and creating a loyal following of customers go hand in hand. I want to be very clear on this point: it doesn't take extravagant measures and impressing the customer with every interaction to create loyalty. You do want to look for opportunities to go above and beyond and wow them when the time presents itself, but you don't have to do that all of the time. It's virtually impossible to do that with every customer all the time! What is possible is doing the little things that make a customer feel valuable and important consistently.

Remember that creating a loyal following of customers sets up your future success.

"

**Don't worry about failures, worry about the
chances you miss when you don't even try.**

JACK CANFIELD

CHAPTER 7:
THE #1 REASON

Have you ever felt *super* appreciated?

Maybe you were recognized and honored for an achievement? Maybe your family or friends thanked you for your help. At some point in your life, you've felt appreciated. How exactly did being appreciated make you feel? Happy? Important? Special? All of the above? Being appreciated makes us feel good about ourselves and we want and need that.

Customers just want to be appreciated for doing business with you. The primary reason a customer will leave a business is that they feel unappreciated.

un·ap·pre·ci·at·ed

adjective
not fully understood, recognized, or valued.

Feeling unappreciated is why we leave. We leave jobs, spouses, churches, service clubs and friendships over this awful feeling. Being unappreciated is an indicator of imbalance in relationships. One person feels that they bring more or do more for the relationship and that it isn't reciprocated. Some people will stop giving, hoping others will realize how much they give.

They crave acknowledgment. Some will choose the opposite strategy and give *even more* hoping to receive praise. Others will just walk away, hoping that their absence will be noticed and that they will be missed. If appreciation never comes, the relationship will end.

There is some subjectivity to how people like to be appreciated. I've worked with people who hate being recognized publicly for what they do. A simple and private thank you is enough for them. Others need a public declaration of every little action they take because it makes them feel validated. Everyone is different and how they need appreciation expressed is too.

Your customer wants and needs to feel appreciated in some way. They are fulfilling their part by giving you their money for your product or service. When the customer does their part, they <u>expect</u> the business to show appreciation. This is Customer Service 101. Almost every business will say they know this, but the studies (Bain and Company) show otherwise. This lack of awareness is due to a perception issue and an appreciation issue. As the customer's perception of your customer service is driven by how you make them feel, you have to know whether they feel appreciated or not.

A business with a mediocre product or service can still succeed if they are making everyone feel appreciated! You've probably done business with a company that doesn't have the best product or service, but they just make you feel great. You might even look forward to doing business with them because you feel so appreciated! The opposite is also likely true. I've given up on a great product from a business when I just felt badly about being there.

The customer can fire you and your business whenever they want, and without them you don't even have a business. How do you keep them from firing your business? You constantly and continually make the customer feel appreciated.

66

The best revenge is massive success.

FRANK SINATRA

CHAPTER 8:
CUSTOMER SERVICE MYTHS - BUSTED!

When I speak of customer service myths, I'm referring to the excuses that many business owners and leaders give about why customer service improvement isn't needed in their business. Unfortunately, these myths are a great deterrent to growth and profit.

MYTH #1 – IT'S IMPOSSIBLE TO PROVIDE GREAT CUSTOMER SERVICE ALL OF THE TIME

Planning, developing, training, implementing and monitoring customer service can seem overwhelming and like an impossible task for many business owners and leaders. If they feel this way, they more than likely will never create a customer service culture. When we feel an activity is too big or too difficult, there's a good possibility we won't even try.

The most common hurdles for developing a service culture are:

The Ownership Isn't 100% Committed To The Idea Of Improving Customer Service.

If the ownership and upper management of the company aren't on board, then it becomes very difficult to transform the business. Businesses function from the top down, and ultimately, whatever the top's attitude is will trickle down to the rest of the company. If the top isn't dedicated to making customer service a priority, then you're fighting an uphill battle.

They Haven't Hired The Right People.

Hiring is critical for every business in terms of its customer service. It's problematic when companies hire too many employees that are experienced and technically great but lack a friendly personality. Employees don't all necessarily have to be superstars or have a bubbly personality. There needs to be a good balance of people. My first rule in hiring is: *Hire Attitude and Train the Rest.*

They Aren't Consistent In Performing The Proper Actions.

Consistency in everything is what ultimately creates success. Inconsistent customer service will plague a company even as they are trying to make improvements. I call this the "Shiny New Object Syndrome." A new idea, concept, piece of equipment or technology can create a bunch of exciting initial plans, and it's very exciting to launch. After a few days, weeks, or months, however, the excitement wears off. Everyday business has to be attended to and the new shiny object is not the central focus anymore. It isn't sustainable. Commitment and consistency are the real tools needed. It's like any of us trying to learn a new skill. If we are committed and consistent and we power through the difficult early stages, we eventually get better and better, and develop to the point of proficiency – if not mastery. It's like the saying that everything is difficult before it becomes easy.

Customer service is not that difficult to implement or improve, especially if you understand the incredible benefits of doing so. The concepts I coach with my clients are very simple. When these ideas and actions are put into place, great customer service moves from the impossible to the possible.

MYTH #2 – ADVERTISING IS MORE IMPORTANT THAN CUSTOMER SERVICE

Here are some interesting and eye-opening statistics I continually refer my clients to and I'll reference throughout this book:

> *It costs a business 5 to 25 times more money to acquire a new customer than to keep an established customer.*

> *A 5% improvement in customer service and retention can lead to a 25% to 95% increase in profits. (The 5% Bump)*

These two statistics should be enough to dispel this myth forever and it basically boils down to one of two thoughts:

> *Do I spend a bunch of money trying to attract new customers who won't continue to buy consistently because my customer service stinks?*

Or

> *Do I spend a little bit of money improving customer service and keep my customers coming back and increase my profits from 25% to 95% over time?*

I'm continually surprised by how many businesses buy into this myth and follow it like gospel. They keep throwing money into marketing to attract new business, yet their business never grows or at best, it's a very slow increase that takes even more money to stimulate. This is often called "organic growth." If you spend enough on advertising and pushing in new business, you can keep a few of those customers coming back. It won't be because they are loyal to the business, but because they haven't been seduced by a competitor with a better offer. This goes back to the satisfied customer who has a wandering eye and will leave your business for any reason. It's not a question of if they will leave, it's when they will leave.

What continues to astonish me is that with overwhelming information, studies, surveys and statistics showing the incredible benefits of improved customer service, many businesses still fail to see the importance of great customer service and continue to focus on improving other areas that will never have the ROI that great customer service offers. I have talked to many business owners who are wholly focused on advertising and the constant need for new customers, and I find they never step back and look at the big picture. They don't understand why those same new customers are leaving their business in droves.

Advertising is important. It's the truth. But relying solely on advertising to grow and sustain business is short-sighted. It is more important to do everything you can to keep those customers coming back. The quickest and most effective way to keep customers coming back is to provide exceptional customer service. The numbers never lie.

MYTH #3 – MY BUSINESS ALREADY PROVIDES GREAT CUSTOMER SERVICE

Of all the myths, this is the most common. This myth reminds me of how most males think they're great drivers. The problem is that insurance companies and statistics say otherwise.

At best, the majority of businesses provide mediocre, watered-down customer service. Business owners often deceive themselves that because they have a few pieces of great customer service in place, it qualifies as exceptional service. This gives them a false sense of security. The reality is they don't see the areas of service they fall short on that are causing them to lose customers and money.

You have to always remember that what the owner or management perceives and what the customer perceives as great customer service are often very different realities. Customer perception is everything. That's why this myth is so concerning to me. To make improvements here means breaking down these delusions. Many business owners never realize that their service is costing them a lot of customers and profit. Evaluative feedback from coaching and consultants is the only way for these businesses to shift course.

66

There is no person living who isn't capable of doing more than he thinks he can do.

HENRY FORD

CHAPTER 9:
CUSTOMERS SERVICE KILLERS

At times, it's better to know what not to do as opposed to what to do.

On my first day at that landscaping company, the crew boss handed me an industrial weed eater and said: "Don't tear up the grass or the plants." Then, using much more colorful language, he told me to get to work.

I learned very quickly how to use the machine with that singular instruction in mind... don't tear up the grass or plants... I didn't know exactly what to do, but I knew exactly what *not* to do and I was instantly a valuable employee.

The same can hold true for your business with your customer service. Grand gestures intended to wow your customers might seem like a good plan, but in reality, it's hard to wow your customers all the time and those gestures don't always impress as much as you might think they do. There are, however, very specific actions you can take, and when done consistently, they will make your customer feel valued and important.

Do these two things to immediately improve your level of customer service:

1. Make your customer feel like the most important person every single time they do business with you. This is the philosophy behind this book.

2. Just as I learned from my first job: Figure out what *not* to do.

THE TOP FIVE CUSTOMER SERVICE KILLERS

How will a pretty good customer service experience turn into a bad one in a matter of seconds? Why is knowing what not to do so important? Here are a couple of statistics that will help to answer these questions.

It takes twelve great customer experiences to make up for one bad customer experience. (Ruby Newell-Legner's "Understanding Customers")

Even worse, 51% of customers won't do business with a company again after one bad experience. Ninety-two percent will leave after two or three negative interactions! You won't get another chance to make things right.

It's human nature to remember the negative and that's exactly what happens with customers. It doesn't matter if there are hundreds of positive things you do because your customers will only remember the one negative thing they experienced.

I've benefited from having great coaches guide me along my professional career. I'm a big believer in coaching and I'm still working with coaches today. The great thing about a coach is that they can offer an outside perspective. They are objective in their assessment of a business and what should or shouldn't be done. They also aren't as emotionally involved as you might be. Coaches have seen what works for others. They know why businesses struggle. They have a wealth of knowledge about what to do and especially what not to do.

People generally learn lessons in two ways: making their own mistakes and learning from the mistakes of others. Effective coaching helps you avoid mistakes, which will save you a great deal of time and money. I can offer my clients proactive steps to improve their business, but often the best insights are gained from hearing about the mistakes I've helped others to navigate and about the mistakes I've also made along the way.

So, what are these mistakes?

NOT BEING FRIENDLY CONSISTENTLY

Have you ever met someone who you might want to be in a relationship with and the first time you met, there seemed to be a real connection, but later, when you contacted them again, they acted like you never existed?

That's very similar to how a consumer feels when a business is friendly one time but not the next or when some employees are friendly and some aren't. It's like being ghosted in a relationship! It can be very confusing and discouraging for a consumer. When a consumer feels unappreciated, they won't be a customer for very long. This is common among new small businesses. They start off super friendly when they are excited about their new venture, but then when the newness wears off and the daily reality of running a business sets in, the friendliness of the staff declines. A great way to disrespect a customer is to not be friendly or to be inconsistently friendly.

HAVING A DIRTY, MESSY AND DISORGANIZED BUSINESS

Have you ever watched an episode of the show *Hoarders*? The premise of the show is for a family member or close friend of the hoarder to intervene and save the person from all the things they've accumulated. Typically, their house is a complete disaster filled from floor to ceiling with things and filth.

Imagine if you walked into a business that looked similar to a house on *Hoarders* and how it would make you feel. Even if the business has phenomenal customer service, they will lose many customers because the look of the business is a mess. No business owner wants to lose customers for any reason, but especially for one that is fairly easy to fix.

In my clinics, anywhere a patient could see had to be clean and organized, including the outside of the building. Most shoppers say that the exterior appearance of a business influences whether or not they will shop there. Having a dirty or untidy business makes a very distinct impression in the customer's mind. It will make them question the quality of everything associated with the business, including the service, handling and the product. It puts doubt into the customer's mind. Never underestimate the power of a clean, neat and organized business.

SLOW DELIVERY OF YOUR SERVICE OR PRODUCT

Before I stopped eating fast food many years ago, I would frequent a particular restaurant chain because of its proximity to my office. Going through the drive-thru was an unpredictable experience because you never knew how fast or slow the service would be. Some days it would be quick like you would expect a fast-food restaurant to be, and other days it would be unbearably slow. Twice I waited in the drive-thru line for over 30 minutes for my order. Their Drive-thru lane was curbed with landscaping and I was effectively trapped in the queue. After the second experience of waiting over 30 minutes, I never went back.

We live in a microwave society. We want everything instantly. I'm not judging this as right or wrong. It's just the way it is, and it will likely continue to be that way. From a business standpoint, you can either embrace this and provide great and quick service, or you can suffer the consequences of losing customers.

People want what they want, when they want it, and without a wait. If you consistently make customers wait when they feel they shouldn't, you will lose them. Remember, great customer service is based on what customers perceive, so if their perception is that your service is slow, then that is the reality.

Consistency plays a huge part in this perception. Just like my experience with the fast-food restaurant, if your service is fast one day and much slower the next, that will be an issue for your customers. You need to address this in your procedures.

The bottom line is that you want to be as expedient in your service to your customers as possible. Depending on your business and industry, customers have expectations of what fast or slow service should be. Your job is to understand those expectations and not only meet them – but try to exceed them if possible. The key is to continually look for ways to speed your processes and service and make it more convenient for the customer. I'll address this in more detail in an upcoming chapter.

NOT TAKING RESPONSIBILITY FOR MISTAKES

Mistakes happen. It's a part of business and life and they're unavoidable. For me, some of the most difficult people to get along with are those who won't own up to their mistakes and blame others for them.

The same holds true for businesses. The ones that can't own up to their mistakes and place the blame on something or someone else are the businesses that lose customers at a rapid rate. In my clinics, I trained my staff to immediately own up to a mistake and to apologize for it. We did this even if the problem wasn't necessarily 100% our fault. If it was our fault, then it was even more important to apologize and rectify the situation quickly to make the customer happy. When my staff learned to immediately apologize for our missteps, the patients were pleasantly shocked to realize that our objective was always to make things right. We were not there to play the blame game and escalate the situation. There are no winners in the blame game.

When a business openly and immediately admits to a mistake, resolves it quickly, and does whatever it takes to satisfy the customer, this helps to create loyal customers who are raving fans. Conversely, when a business won't take responsibility for a mistake, blames others, and doesn't budge on rectifying the situation with a customer, it creates a completely different kind of referral. There's an adage that says, "you can be right or you can be happy." I'd rather suck up my pride, admit my mistakes, create an ultra-successful business and be happy. How about you?

INADEQUATE OR LACKING COMMUNICATION

"Communication is the bridge between confusion and clarity."
                                                            -Nat Turner

Communication plays a critical role in every area of our lives and our relationships. This is never more evident than in the realm of business (and marriage).

A confused customer won't be a customer for long. Admittedly, I did a poor job in my early chiropractic career with communicating to my patients and employees. I lost patients and employees regularly. Through coaching and reflection, I realized my poor communication was causing most of my problems. I made it my goal and mantra to communicate and communicate – and then communicate some more! Obviously, this made a positive impact on retaining patients and employees.

Communication can seem daunting and overwhelming. You'll find in your business there are only a few key questions that customers will need to have addressed regularly. When you address those key topics fully, you reduce the need for further follow-up and continued clarification. As a chiropractor, if I explained what a patient's condition was, explained if and how we could treat it, specified how long the treatment would take, and estimated how much it would cost, the patient would have most of their questions answered.

Never underestimate the importance of communication with your customers and employees. Identify the critical questions and create a system to address them proactively, before the customer even knows to ask. I coach my clients to over-communicate. Over-communicating is telling the customer the same details over and over - as often as it takes for them to understand. When you think the customer understands, you tell them some more! You don't do this in a demeaning way. You do it with a smile as if it's the first time you've explained it. The customer will let you know when they completely understand. My clients worry their customers will tire of hearing the same information, but customers have a million other things on their minds. Communicating with a customer and with employees should always be done with a *serving* mindset and to make the customer feel valued.

66

Successful people are simply those with successful habits.

BRIAN TRACY

CHAPTER 10:
GETTING BETTER OR GETTING WORSE.
THERE IS NO NEUTRAL.

For 20 years, I loved taking care of patients and helping them lead healthier lives. I would often tell my patients: "There is no neutral to health." Either you're doing things making you healthier or you're doing things keeping you from being healthy. This would help them to better understand the concept of health. Most patients and people base their health on their symptoms and if they are in pain or having dysfunction in their body. It's very important to monitor and recognize symptoms, but it's a reactive way to live. Many people do very little to get and stay healthy. They react to their symptoms and expect to remedy them with drugs or surgery. This is the American way. Proactive healthcare is doing the things that make you healthier to lessen the likelihood of health issues. This doesn't guarantee you won't have problems, but in general, they're less severe and easier to remedy the healthier you are.

Many businesses are run in the same reactive way that people deal with their health. They don't realize that there's no neutral in business success. In other words, you're getting better or you're getting worse. You never stay the same. Either the business is doing the things to grow and improve or they're doing the same old same old and coasting along. The funny thing about coasting is you can only go one direction. Downhill. My first business coach would often say: "You're either green and growing, or ripe and rotting." I took that to heart and let that philosophy guide me throughout my chiropractic career – and it still guides me as a coach and consultant today.

You want to always be on the lookout for ways to improve your service and processes to make things easier and more convenient for the customer to do business with you. How can you be more efficient? How can you excite the customer? In what ways can you help your customers to feel more valued and important? Ask these questions regularly, or work with a consultant who will challenge you to review your service regularly.

Many businesses are reactive to customer service. They realize there's a problem or symptom but instead of trying to understand the true *cause* they have a knee-jerk reaction and look for the Band-Aids. Or worse, they attempt to overhaul everything. This is usually incredibly time-consuming and expensive. The better method is to find the underlying cause of service breakdown and make strategic changes.

For business, in health, and in life in general, there is no neutral. You're either actively trying to improve or you're not. Sometimes, we're slow to initiate good habits when there's no immediate symptom telling us to. Dedicating yourself to constantly improve, and to be brilliant at the basics will create service that your customers will feel very loyal to support.

"

My biggest motivation? Just to keep challenging myself. I see life almost like one long university education that I never had - every day I'm learning something new.

SIR RICHARD BRANSON

CHAPTER 11:
THE 3 F'S (BACK TO THE BASICS)

Because I value simplicity, I am a huge advocate of getting back to the basics. Throughout my chiropractic career, I have always benefited from a review of the rudimentary procedures. I regularly attended seminars and sought counsel to help me to keep the basics in check.

When we stray from the basics, we lose sight of what helped to create our success in the first place. This is certainly true in sports. If a team is in the middle of a losing streak, they'll have a team meeting and re-commit to the basics. When reminded of what made them successful, they're soon to be winning again. Running a business can be the same way. If the numbers are slipping, call a team meeting. Define the basics. Success is sure to follow.

I teach my clients what I learned through my years of practice. One of the best ways to improve service is to get back-to-basics. When I was just starting, I constantly looked for ways to make a better experience for my patients. Occasionally, I would get so focused on improving things we would forget some of the very basic actions! When doing system evaluations, I was occasionally surprised by some of the simple things we let fall through the cracks. These little things made a big difference in making a lasting impression in the customer's mind.

You always have to remember what got you to where you're at will help to keep you where you're at. You can likely innovate and improve, but it's also vital to *continue* doing the little things that helped create the success of your business in the first place. When consulting with clients, we track the basics. It's easy to get caught up in reacting to problems. When a commitment to get back-to-basics is made, it often turns their season around. The 3 F's are the basics:

FRIENDLY

Being friendly is the most basic customer service action. Every employee, with every customer, every day, should be as friendly as possible. Friendliness should be the common theme from start to finish and everywhere between with customer interactions. Being friendly sets the stage for the customer and gives them the sense they are appreciated and valuable to the business. Friendliness goes a long way toward accomplishing that goal.

FAST

We are used to instant gratification. The quicker a business takes hold of this reality and works it to their advantage, the better. Customers expect businesses to accommodate them quickly in every aspect of their experience. It serves a business well to look at its processes and procedures to determine where they may be slow in serving the customer, and then streamline that process.

One area I feel businesses often drop the ball in being fast is with follow-up messaging. When a customer is relying on timely communication and is promised a call when the service is complete, there's going to be a problem if messages are delayed.

It's no good to call in and hear "I was just about to call you." This is a symptom of a business attitude.

FIXING PROBLEMS (SERVICE RECOVERY)

Mistakes happen all the time in business. Some are large, some small, some are easier than others to fix. When there's a breakdown, the business makes a choice. They either fix the issue to the satisfaction of the business or the satisfaction of the customer. When a business fixes issues to the satisfaction of the customer, it creates incredible loyalty.

The 3 F's are where we start and restart. Which one should you focus on?

PART THREE:
DELIVER IT

66

Act as if it were impossible to fail.

DOROTHEA BRANDE

CHAPTER 12:
EMPLOYEE RELATIONSHIPS (DON'T MESS THIS UP)

Happy Employee = Happy Customer (Most of the Time)

The biggest challenge I faced with improving the customer service in my office was learning how to better handle my employees. Admittedly, it was 100% my fault. It took me a long time to grasp the idea that when my employees are happy, they are more likely to make the patients happy. It's a very simple concept to remember, the happier the employees are, the happier the customers will be.

How can you create a positive relationship with employees that will make them happier, and will inspire them to do the job they were hired to do? It's surprisingly very easy. You will need to cultivate respect and teamwork. This chapter is dedicated to helping you understand how to show respect for your employees and how to honor the team.

Let's start with respecting employees, which also results in reciprocal respect for you as the employer. I'm a firm believer that our inner game creates our outer circumstances. If a business owner lacks self-confidence and suffers from feelings of inferiority, it will ultimately be on display. Typically, it shows up as micromanagement from an overbearing, never-wrong boss. It is very difficult to lead employees this way and it is ultimately very dispiriting and counterproductive. This behavior creates resentment and your employees won't want to do the work right, if at all. The relationship the employer creates with the employees begins and ends with the employer's *attitude*. We can control our thoughts and attitudes and it is critical to do so when leading a team of employees.

I wasn't the kind of employer I should have been for many years. My mindset was that employees were a liability and that they always had to be monitored and corrected. I believed that if I slacked in my monitoring of the employees, they would do whatever they wanted, and not what was required. My monitoring reinforced the idea that they were a liability, only collecting a paycheck, and doing the bare minimum. You can guess what kind of office environment I created. There was little respect, and it was a me-vs-them situation. Before you judge me too harshly, I'll tell you I wasn't a tyrant ruling with an iron fist. I had a few employees work with me for years, and even some that came back as patients after their employment ended. So, there were *some* things that I did right. They weren't completely miserable!

What changed the dynamic of the relationships I had with my employees was when I viewed them as *assets and* looked for the good they were doing. As it turns out, the good far outweighed the bad! I honored them as vital components to our success. I realized they did a ton of great things I needed to acknowledge! Just a few examples of these great things were their friendliness and great personalities. They would come in early and stay late. They would go above and beyond often for the patients without being asked. This was an absolute game-changer and helped us to advance our clinics to the next level.

As my attitude shifted toward my employees, they developed a better attitude toward me (shocker). My employees seemed to enjoy being at work and our patients could see this! Happy employee, happy customer. And now, my employees were doing all of the things that needed to get done without hesitation. As I continued to see their efforts and acknowledge them, it motivated them to do their work well, which created mutual respect, which engendered their confidence in me. We built a fulfilling working relationship.

To create better, respectful relationships with employees:

1. Think of the employees as assets. They are there to help the business succeed.
2. Actively and consistently look for the good that your employees do. Stop focusing on the mistakes.
3. Praise the employees publicly for their great work regularly.

These three simple actions will make a tremendous shift in the atmosphere of your business.

HIRE ATTITUDE AND TRAIN THE REST

Great working relationships begin with the hiring process. Even when we develop a system for hiring meant to narrow down the candidates to discover the best possible candidate for the job, we can still hire someone just plain wrong for the job. I've been advised by most of my business coaches to hire slow and fire fast. I've discovered better tactics: hire fast and fire fast. Try to hire a great person that fits the criteria you have, but use your gut feeling to get someone hired. My number-one rule for hiring is: Hire Attitude and Train the Rest. I'd much rather have an upbeat, smiling, enthusiastic employee I have to train on the technology than the opposite scenario.

THE TWO-WEEK RULE

In my practice, I gave new hires two weeks to show me their stuff. I believe in going with my gut here as well. I can generally tell if an employee will work out within two weeks. If I felt like they weren't a good fit, I would let them go. This may seem harsh, but I put up with too many bad employees for way too long and learned it's better to nip it in the bud. A wrong hire creates stress and negativity, killing the positive atmosphere needed for exceptional customer service.

TRAINING TACTICS

Great training makes for great employee performance. Training has to be done consistently and ongoing. Many businesses train employees when they're initially hired and then that is all the training ever done. Regular training will reinforce the ideas and actions needed to run the business, and it also gives employees confidence as they develop their skills. How we train our employees is equally important. Every employee makes mistakes. Failure is part of the learning process. It's up to the boss to address and correct mistakes when they happen. I have three rules for correcting and criticizing employees:

Never criticize or correct when you're angry.

> When emotions run high, reason runs low. When upset, you're much more likely to say things that shouldn't be said. You risk criticizing the person instead of the action needing to be addressed. It's important to give yourself enough time to calm down and regroup before you speak with the employee. This may be a minute or two, a few hours, or a day. Whatever time you need to become calmer and more rational is very important and will save you trouble down the line. This should be a rule for any relationship, by the way.

Praise in public and criticize in private.

> Never criticize an employee in front of anyone, especially other employees, and definitely not your customers. It's humiliating enough to be criticized in private, but to have it done in front of others is a self-esteem destroyer. It's best to take the employee aside into a private space when you are not angry and discuss the issue. Be specific about what needs to be changed. It only takes a few minutes and, although unpleasant, the employee's self-esteem will still be intact.

Use the Compliment Sandwich Method.

> Sandwich the criticism in-between two compliments about what the employee does well. Point out something good they are doing, then bring up the issue to be worked on and corrected, and then finish with another compliment. This takes the sting off of being corrected and bolsters their self-esteem. When you've helped the employee understand and correct an issue while saving face and maintaining self-esteem, it's a win-win for the business and the employee. Again, when employees are treated with respect, they will be in a better place to provide exceptional customer service. Happy employee, happy customer!

BUILDING THE TEAM

I'm a huge sports fan, so I like to use sports analogies to describe what I mean. In professional football, everyone in the organization supports the team so they can succeed and win games. There are many parts to a football team: the coaches, trainers, players, support personnel, and countless others. It takes all kinds of people in various positions to make a successful team. The most successful teams live by their team identity. These teams' value all of its players, believing that everyone is vital to their shared success. Some people certainly get paid more and get more recognition, but the truly great teams honor the importance of every person involved.

In my offices, I made sure everyone knew they were valuable to the success of our business. I had different employee types (associate doctors, office managers, full-time and part-time assistants). They were all paid differently with their different titles, but I maintained the concept that everyone was important and played a big part in the success of our business. I communicated this regularly to all of the employees. This was especially important to the lower-level employees doing the unpleasant tasks that needed to be done. When they felt that what they were doing mattered, it gave them a sense of pride. They didn't want to let the team down.

Fostering the team concept also helps to keep egos and attitudes in check. If everyone is on board and understands the importance of everyone else, then it keeps the people that have earned the right to be a manager or boss from thinking they are the most important piece in the business puzzle and from treating others disrespectfully. Yes, they may have greater responsibility, but not greater importance.

I can't stress enough the importance of respecting your employees and building a team atmosphere with them. Thinking you can treat your employees badly and then expecting them to give great customer service is flawed logic. It just won't work! You might be able to get them to go through the motions and to give decent service, but it will never be as good as it should be or could be. Remember, the way you treat your employees is the way they will treat your customers.

66

Action is the foundational key to all success.

ANTHONY ROBBINS

CHAPTER 13:
IT ALL HAS TO BE RIGHT

Have you ever had this happen to you?

You go out to eat at one of your favorite restaurants and you get seated right away. The server greets you quickly and your order is brought to your table in a timely manner. You finish a great meal and ask the server for the check. And then it takes an exceptionally long time to get the check, get the payment processed, and get your receipt and a thank you?

Or perhaps, you've gone through the drive-thru at a fast-food restaurant. You order, pay, and get your items very quickly. You drive home to enjoy your meal with your family. Then at home, you discover an item is missing?

We've all experienced scenarios like these. A customer can have an experience with a business where most of the experience is great, but a bit of the experience goes completely wrong. When this happens, what do you think the customer remembers? They remember the part of the experience that went wrong. Customers focus on the negative in every experience.

This is why every aspect of customer service has to be good because your customer service will be judged by its weakest link.

You can't afford to have weak links because it will cost you. Unfortunately, for many businesses, there are often multiple weak links that need to be addressed. The grand gestures intended to impress the customers don't mean a thing without consistent performance. This is the unofficial theme of this book. From start to finish the service for every customer must be consistently good. The customer's perception is what matters most.

The quickest and easiest way to find out where there is a problem and weak link in your service is to learn from the customers directly. Most customers, when surveyed or asked, don't want to hurt anyone's feelings so they'll just say everything is great. Occasionally, a customer will get irritated enough they will make a complaint. Customers who give the best information, however, are those that left the business and didn't complain. Those are the customers you can get the best information from about a weak area of customer service. Surveying the customers who disappeared is your best resource for discovering service breakdowns and problems.

The little lapses in your service cause real havoc in your business. What is happening that you aren't seeing? What is the perception of your previous customer?

Problems happen, mistakes happen, and people get offended occasionally. This is human nature. When these issues happen, they are a *golden opportunity* to make things right! If these issues happen regularly and are never addressed, real damage occurs. It's tough to bounce back from that.

66

If you don't like how things are, change it! You're not a tree.

JIM ROHN

CHAPTER 14:
THE ART OF MAKING THINGS RIGHT

The unfortunate things, the slips-ups, mess-ups and goof-ups happen. These foul-ups can either be handled in a very positive or negative way for the customer. When a business corrects a wrong the right way, the customer is much more likely to remain a fan and be extremely loyal to the business. I can attest to this. Some of the best and most loyal patients I had in my clinic became that way because we corrected an error and made things right for them. They become a walking-and-talking advertisement for my office and a constant referral source. The choice is very clear on this: either you do what's convenient for the business or you do what's right for the customer. It's easy to say customer service is important when everything is running smoothly and you have no complaints or problems. The businesses that stand out are the ones that take care of all customers' complaints or problems in an extraordinary way.

In this chapter, I want to share with you the formula for taking care of the slighted, upset or complaining customer. Knowing what to do and having a plan before the problem arises is half the battle. Many businesses don't have a plan and don't train their front-line employees properly to deal with complaints and issues. Have you ever been the customer voicing an issue or complaint and the employee or customer service rep acts like they have never dealt with a complaint or problem before? They act like no customer had *ever* had a problem before, so they don't know exactly what to do or *if* they can do anything at all. Again, knowing there will be problems and then having a plan to deal with the problems will pay off many times over.

NEVER PLAY THE BLAME GAME

The first step in the making things right formula is to never play the blame game. No one wins and this will result in losing a customer. You may have seen this at work in relationships. Blame your partner or friend for something and see what it gets you. No one wants to be blamed for anything, even if it was blatantly their fault. Sometimes when a customer has an issue or something has gone wrong in their experience with a business, it is 100% the customer's fault. At this point, the business has a choice. It can point out the fault and demean the customer or the business can act like the problem is common it happens all the time and help the customer to save face. Pride is a strong force in all our lives and our natural instinct is to protect it at all costs. When a business takes the stance of protecting its pride when the problem was initiated by the business, it is incredibly damaging to customer relationships.

APOLOGIZE NO MATTER WHAT

When an apology is given quickly, it helps to calm the customer and defuse the situation.

> *What if it's <u>clearly</u> the customer's fault?*
> *Why should the business apologize?*
> *Won't we be lying?*

Remember – don't play the blame game no matter what and even if the customer is wrong they're still your customer. There are ways to apologize that are considerate but don't assign blame. You can use these phrases when it's clearly the customers fault:

> *I'm so sorry this happened.*
> *I'm so sorry you experienced that.*
> *I apologize for the trouble this has caused you.*
> *That is horrible, let's get this fixed for you.*

The key is empathy.

em·pa·thy

noun
1 the ability to understand and share the feelings of another.

The point is to make the customer feel important and that the business is there for them and showing empathy does just that. Taking pride and blame out of the equation allows space for empathy to shine through. If the business is clearly at fault, empathy is still needed for the upset customer and an apology should be immediately given taking full responsibility. You can say:

> *I'm so sorry we dropped the ball on this.*
> *I apologize for messing this up and causing inconvenience for you.*
> *We will do whatever we can to make it right for you.*

This last statement is one of the most powerful you can say. Often you'll hear a *"let me see what I can do"* which is better than nothing, but it rarely does enough to create complete confidence in the customer's mind.

No matter who is at fault, an apology should be given by the business to show empathy and/or to shoulder responsibility.

DO WHATEVER IT TAKES TO SATISFY THE CUSTOMER

A simple way to find out what will satisfy the customer is to ask them!

> *How can we make this right?*
> *How can we make this up to you?*
> *What would make you happy?"*

Most customers will give you a reasonable request. Obviously, there will be those few who will try to take advantage of the situation and demand much more than the situation dictates. They may try to see how much they can get, so they ask for the moon. You can acknowledge the request and still come to a compromise that will be appropriate. For the vast majority of customers, all they want is to be rightly compensated and will give reasonable requests or demands. What may seem like a loss to the company because of the mess-up can ultimately be turned into a huge gain when a problem is handled correctly. You have the opportunity to spend a little for a mess-up to potentially gain a loyal customer that refers others to your business. This can be a fantastic return on investment.

RESOLVE COMPLAINTS QUICKLY

I've been married for 20+ years to the love of my life. I've learned through the years that an immediate answer is required of me in certain situations. For example, if my wife is trying on some clothing and asks, *"Does this dress look good on me?"*, my answer must be immediate! If I hesitate for any length of time, even if I answer positively, it doesn't really matter what I say because my wife will interpret meaning from the silence.

The very same scenario happens with customers. Any delay in addressing an issue will leave a bad taste in the customer's mouth. The customer will interpret a lack of urgency as indifference, or worse, that the company is trying to get away with the mistake. The customer will appreciate the effort to right a wrong but will remember the lack of immediate attention. You don't want to give the customer the opportunity to make a BUT statement: *"They did take care of my problem, BUT it took them forever to do so."* We always want the customer to have an AND statement: *"The business really took care of my problem AND they did it without hesitation."* When the business knows it made a mistake and apologizes before the customer even knows there's a problem, it makes an incredible impression and gives the customer full confidence that the business is fully committed to serving them.

When the heat is on with an upset customer, the true colors of a business come shining through. This is your opportunity to stand head and shoulders above your competition and blow the customer away by how you take care of a problem. Never underestimate the power or the importance in the art of making things right.

The Making it Right Formula:
- Never play the blame game
- Apologize no matter what
- Do whatever it takes to satisfy the customer
- Resolve complaints quickly

"

Everything you want is just outside your comfort zone.

ROBERT G. ALLEN

CHAPTER 15:
ENTHUSIASM AND A POSITIVE MENTAL ATTITUDE

Enthusiasm and a Positive Mental Attitude (PMA) play a large part in all successes in life. Let's look closely at how enthusiasm and a PMA relate to exceptional customer service.

ENTHUSIASM

en·thu·si·asm

noun
1 intense and eager enjoyment, interest, or approval.

When you're enthusiastic, you want to share your enthusiasm. I'm extremely enthusiastic when my team wins the big game. You've been around family or friends who just found out they are pregnant or engaged. Maybe they just got a promotion or landed a new job. Enthusiasm is contagious. When my kids were little and learned new skills like tying their shoes or riding a bike, they were so enthusiastic. This made my wife and I enthusiastic too. When your employees are enthusiastic about the business, the product, or the service provided, the customer will become more enthusiastic, as well.

Have you ever watched an infomercial and noticed how the host is always over-the-top enthusiastic about the product they are pitching? They understand that the level of their enthusiasm is contagious. The consumer will never be any more enthusiastic about the product than the host. If the host isn't excited, the consumer won't be enthusiastic about making a purchase. In the early days of my chiropractic practice, I got it into my mind for some reason that I needed to be very serious with my patients because health is a serious matter (which it is). The problem was that I focused on the seriousness of the conditions I was treating (which is important) instead of focusing on being enthusiastic about the treatment I gave, which helped the patient get healthier. I finally discovered that if I was enthusiastic about the patient's treatment, the patient was more enthusiastic about their treatment and would be more likely to follow through on their care.

Communication is often non-verbal. Tone of voice and body language are tools for communicating. An enthusiastic person has a lot of energy and excitement.

Your employees should be enthusiastic about the business, the product and, most of all, about serving the customer. Even if the right things are said and done, if energy or enthusiasm are lacking, it won't be very effective. When we moved to Texas, I visited a chain barbershop a few times. When I called to make an appointment, the person who answered the phone sounded like they were upset I called. There was no greeting beyond a perfunctory hello. Their tone was low-energy and negative. After scheduling my haircut, I wasn't offered a positive farewell at the conclusion of the call. Obviously, I wasn't really excited about getting a haircut at that shop. In contrast, there's a supplement company that I've used for years because of their great products. Whenever I call them to place an order, there is always someone who answers the phone that sounds like they are genuinely excited and enthusiastic that I called. They have a friendly greeting and farewell and genuinely sound like they are there to help me in any way they can. Which business do I feel more enthusiastic about? Eventually, I found a different stylist to cut my hair.

Enthusiasm is the Secret Sauce to great customer service. Even a business that isn't really great in their service can be perceived as having decent service if they show tremendous enthusiasm for their customers. The right idea is to combine enthusiasm with great service.

So, how do you develop and sustain enthusiasm? What if you're not feeling it? Sometimes life is tough and we carry that weight with us to work. Monday morning can be a real enthusiasm killer. It's always easier to be enthusiastic on a Friday.

To create enthusiasm, use the "As If Principle." The "As If Principle" is simply this: You act as if you are enthusiastic and by doing so you will become enthusiastic. This principle holds true for any characteristic or emotion you want to exhibit. You just act the way you want to feel and soon enough you'll start feeling that way. There's a direct relationship between our emotions and our physiology. Our bodies and our emotions work together. We can trick our emotions by changing our body language. If you or your employees aren't feeling super-enthusiastic, all you have to do is start acting enthusiastic and the feeling will follow shortly. What does enthusiasm look like in your body? Your head is up, shoulders are back, you're smiling, you're making eye contact, talking a little louder and you're moving a little quicker. I guarantee this works because I have done it hundreds of times and I have seen it work with my employees and clients.

POSITIVE MENTAL ATTITUDE

Friendliness is at the core of great customer service. When the atmosphere of the business is inherently negative, it will be very difficult to be authentically friendly and serve customers. You can put all the great customer service principles and actions into place and do them consistently, but a negative attitude will hamper the best of intentions.

If "positive mental attitude" were in the dictionary:

positive·mental·attitude (PMA)

noun
1 the philosophy of having an optimistic disposition in every situation in one's life to attract positive outcomes.

You reap what you sow. If you're positive and optimistic, you attract the positive and if you're more negative and pessimistic, then that's what you'll attract. Having a PMA helps you look at every situation, whether good or bad and to see the positive or what can be positively attained. So, it's important in life and certainly in business to think about and focus on the positive things.

"We become what we think about most of the time."

-Earl Nightingale

When a sports team is struggling to win a game, the commenter might say: *"They're playing not to lose instead of playing to win."* Some businesses are run this way. They play not to lose what they've got instead of playing to prosper and grow. This kind of scarcity mindset is enforcing the negative, the idea of potential loss.

The very essence of serving someone is a very positive act. It seems pretty obvious, but is not always accomplished. So, how can you help yourself and your employees to develop a PMA? Here are three methods to help create a positive state of mind:

SET YOUR GOALS

Goal setting is a big and juicy topic and the subject of many books. There are many studies on the benefits of goals and how they can help in achieving greater success. A study by the Harvard MBA Business School showed that after ten years, the 3% of their graduates that had written goals and a plan for their attainment made ten times more money than the other 97% of graduates. That's compelling proof about the tremendous power of creating goals. Like developing a PMA, goals keep us focused on what we *want*, not what we don't. And what if what we want is the best for all involved?

"You can have everything in life you want if you help enough others get what they want."

-Zig Ziglar

If your goal is to serve the customer first, you can have what you want through their experience. To achieve your goals, you have to do the work, they just don't magically appear. If you're going to have to work anyway, you might as well be focused and deliberate in your actions to accomplish what you want. Creating goals that focus on serving others is a very potent combination.

FEED YOUR MIND POSITIVE INFORMATION

We are constantly being bombarded with news and information and very little of it is positive. If we're feeding our minds negative, sensational, degrading information then our thoughts will be stimulated by those ideas. It's extremely important to control what we're exposing our minds to on an everyday basis. We need to be very deliberate about feeding our minds positive motivating, inspirational and educational information. This doesn't stop the negative from happening, but it enforces our PMA. If you have a garden, you wouldn't let the weeds grow and feed the plants soft drinks and poison. No, you pull the weeds, and you give the plants water and fertilizer to help them grow. Like a garden, your mind will grow ideas and thoughts. What are you going to feed your mind? Be very intentional in feeding your mind positive information.

POSITIVE AFFIRMATIONS

Have you stopped to listen to what you say to yourself? How do you talk to yourself inside your head? We are our own worst critics!

> *That was stupid!*
> *Nice going idiot!*
> *That was a dumb thing to say.*

We aren't always very nice to ourselves. We wouldn't dare talk to anybody else like we talk to ourselves. The problem with talking to yourself negatively is your subconscious mind hears those words – and then will act on them. It's just doing what it's told. The adage "...*that sticks and stones may break my bones, but words can never hurt me*" is bologna! Negative words do hurt and cause real damage whether someone else says them or you say them to yourself.

Affirmations are powerful. They are essentially positive instructions to your subconscious mind to act upon. Affirmations are a specific way to nourish your mind with positivity to guide your thoughts well. Affirmations are simple, easy to do, and can be done anytime and anywhere and nobody will ever know. You can say them repeatedly until your mind is saturated. There are countless affirmations you can use or you can create on your own.

As an example, here are some of my favorites:

I'm the best!
I like myself!
I can do it!
I'm responsible!
There are no limits to what I can do!

I've said these to myself thousands of times through the years, and while affirmations didn't make my life perfect, they've helped me to create and maintain a PMA and the belief I can accomplish anything.

Enthusiasm is contagious. Follow these ideas to help create a PMA
- Set your goals
- Feed your mind positive information
- Use positive affirmations

66

Accept responsibility for your life. Know that it is you who will get you where you want to go, no one else.

LES BROWN

CHAPTER 16:
SMILE

George Carlin once quipped, "Everyone smiles in the same language." Smiles are universally welcomed. A smile helps to give the impression of friendliness and lets the customer know they are welcome into your business. It's the beginning of a positive interaction. Body language plays a huge role in our communication and smiling is a big part of that.

A smile is inviting and comforting, it says hello without saying the words. Studies have found that smiling reduces the body's response to stress and can lower blood pressure (University of Kansas). Many people have anxiety about going to the doctor. This makes sense because they don't know what their health issue might be and what they may have to do to resolve it. That was often the case with new patients coming to my office. My office staff were trained to always smile. This didn't completely eliminate the anxiety patients had, but had a real calming effect on them.

In my clinics and with my clients, I recommend that a smile be part of the required uniform for every employee. It should be put on and kept on. This includes employees that talk to customers over the phone. A customer can *feel* a smile through the phone in the tone of voice they hear. When a customer called my clinics, our standard greeting when answering was, "*It's a fantastic day at Henry Chiropractic Clinic, this is _____, how can I help you?"* This greeting had to be said with enthusiasm and a smile that the patient could feel. I placed mirrors next to the phones in the office. That way my office staff could see themselves in the mirror and recognize if they were smiling or not!

Speaking of mirrors, you may have heard that the world is like a mirror. It reflects back whatever you give off. If you smile at someone the majority of the time they will smile back. Try it out sometime and just go around smiling and see what happens. People could think you're weird, sure, but the majority of the time they will smile back at you. This works like a charm in a business setting as related to exceptional customer service. When the employees are smiling, it will prompt the customers to smile, which creates a good feeling in them. The immediate impression is this business is welcoming and friendly.

Sometimes, you're not in the mood to smile because you've had a rough day, or things just don't seem to be going right, and the last thing you want to do is smile and be nice to people. This happens to all of us. I was very aware of the things going on in my employee's lives and I knew when they were struggling. I would tell them, *"Don't wait to be happy to smile. Smile to make yourself happy."* We put a smile on our faces no matter what was going on in our lives or in the clinic. We didn't wait until life was perfect (which it never is) or until things were running smoothly. We put a smile on our faces and focused on serving the patients. The great thing was that by putting a smile on our faces, it made us feel happier. The "As If Principle" applies to smiling. How you act physically informs your emotions. To be happy when you are not, smile and it will make you happier.

Never underestimate the power of smiling. Sometimes the simplest ideas make the biggest impact on the customer. Smiling is free and requires very little training to implement. Make smiling a part of your business uniform.

66

There is no passion to be found in playing small - settling for a life that is less than the one you are capable of living."

NELSON MANDELA

CHAPTER 17:
MAKE THE CUSTOMER SAY AND - NOT BUT

Positively or negatively, customers will talk about your business. You can't stop the customer from talking, and if your business provides great service – you want them to talk! You can influence what the customer says by controlling the level of service your business provides. Bad service will cause the customers to say certain things. Good service will too. Control the service and you control the customer report.

WHEN YOU GET A BAD RAP

When the customer talks about their bad experience, they will probably use a BUT statement.

> *The food was great, but the service was so slow.*
> *They have good prices, but the store was a mess.*
> *They serviced my car correctly, but it took 8 hours!*
> *They inspected the damages to my home, but it took 6 weeks to get a check.*

It's human nature to focus on the negative and gossip about the negative. If the customer has an experience with a negative piece to it, they will likely tell someone about it with a "BUT statement.

WHEN YOU SHINE

The opposite of the BUT statement is the AND statement.

> *Their food was fantastic, and their service was unbelievably good. The office staff was so helpful and the place was spotless.*

You want the customers to be so excited that they keep throwing more ANDs in their description. You want them describing the service with AND they did this, AND this – AND THIS! The AND statement generally adds up as a huge positive from the customer. The BUT statement has the neutral nullified by what comes after the BUT. Here, the focus will always be on the negative.

Think about how a customer would describe their experience with your business. Make your business known for great customer service so the customer can only communicate the ANDs not the BUTs.

66

You are what you are and where you are because of what has gone into your mind. You can change what you are and where you are by changing what goes into your mind.

ZIG ZIGLAR

CHAPTER 18:
OVERLY FRIENDLY

The vast majority of business owners will claim they are extremely friendly with their customers. The businesses you deal with regularly probably feel at least semi-friendly. You are likely always greeted and offered some help. They may even ask how your day is going. Technically, they are friendly. But maybe their intention is more about not appearing rude.

People define friendliness in different ways and to varying degrees. Situations will also dictate the kind of friendliness exhibited. A funeral will have different rules for friendliness than a wedding. Different business types will also have different levels of friendliness.

Businesses could be a lot more friendly than they are. They need to upgrade their friendliness from not being rude to being extra friendly. Or, as I like to call it: Overly Friendly.

o·ver·ly

adverb
excessively.

Being Overly Friendly is, in essence, being excessively friendly or being friendly with a purpose. The purpose is to be friendly to every customer, on every occasion, all the time. Many businesses practice reactive friendliness and we do this generally in life. If the customer or person we are interacting with is showing some friendliness, then we will be open to being friendly, but if they're not friendly, we won't be either. The level of friendliness the customer shows is the level the employee will give back. When an employee is being reactively friendly, it creates the possibility for misinterpretation. Being reactively friendly can appear inconsistent, and customers are left to imagine how the employee feels about their presence. And unfortunately, there are also times when an employee won't even be reactively friendly and is just not friendly at all.

The business should be proactive in their friendliness. I trained my staff to acknowledge the patient with a greeting when they walked in the door. We wanted to let the patient know we were excited they came in and that we were ready to serve them. I wanted the patients to feel immediately welcomed and to know they were important to us. We've all had to wait for someone to acknowledge our existence and it feels terrible. Being Overly Friendly gives the impression that we're here for the customer, and not the other way around.

Being Overly Friendly is about being friendly no matter what. It doesn't matter if the customer has a lousy attitude. Whatever attitude the customer arrives with does not affect how they will be treated because the decision has already been made to treat them with friendliness. The customer's perception is driven by how you make them feel and when you treat them in a friendly manner, you make them happier. The objective is to make the customer feel better when they leave than when they came in.

GREET THE CUSTOMER RIGHT AWAY

Employees need to be consciously aware of customers setting foot inside the business and to greet them as soon as possible. That's step one. Step two is to make this greeting energetic. You can't be Overly Friendly and not be energetic. A greeting that sounds like Eeyore from Winnie the Pooh doesn't do the job. Energy is key. Here are some examples of terrific greetings.

> *Good morning!/ Good afternoon!*
> *Hello, it's great to see you!*
> *Welcome!*
> *Hello, we're glad you're here!*
> *Hello!*

Depending on the business, it might be appropriate to ask, *"How can I help you?"* Or *"What can I do for you today?."* It's helpful to use their name if it's a returning customer. When the customer feels remembered, this makes the greeting even more impactful. A greeting done immediately, with enthusiasm and energy creates a positive impression for a new customer and reinforces it with a returning customer. It's important to make that great first impression and set the tone for the rest of the experience.

GIVE THEM YOUR SMILE

Remember that body language is a huge part of what is communicated. If an immediate and enthusiastic greeting is given without a smile, it won't feel as welcoming. The smile is the universal greeting. You're always working to make the most impactful impression. Combine an enthusiastic greeting with a huge smile and this can have a dramatic effect on making the customer feel special and welcomed.

MAKE EYE CONTACT

It's difficult to communicate with someone who doesn't make eye contact with you. It just doesn't feel right. If you walk into a store and the clerk says hello but never looks up from their phone or what they're working on, it can be perceived as unfriendly. Making eye contact plays a big part in being Overly Friendly.

How Employees Can Be Proactively Overly Friendly:
- Greet the customer right away
- Smile at the customer
- Make eye contact with the customer

"

The person who goes the farthest is
generally the one who is willing to do and
dare. The sure-thing boat never gets far
from shore.

DALE CARNEGIE

CHAPTER 19:
MANNERS MATTER

I grew up in an era where I was taught to use my manners at all times. I learned to say please and thank you, to hold the door open, and to address my elders as Mr. and Mrs. When I was ten years old, I made the mistake of calling my friend's dad by his first name in front of my father. My father let me know in no uncertain terms I was never to do that again and I can honestly say I never did.

These ideas don't seem as important as they once were. The aim of using manners is to show respect to others. Who doesn't want to feel respected? It never hurts to show respect to others in any setting, but it can hurt not to do so. From a customer service standpoint, showing respect helps to reinforce our principle that we want our customer to feel important and valued. When customers feel respected, it stands out because it is becoming a rarer experience.

THE FIVE POWER PHRASES OF MANNERS

Please.
Thank you.
You're welcome.
Yes, please.
No, thank you.

These phrases communicate respect and are very simple to use. And yet, they are so simple they are often neglected. Now that much of our communication is done through text or email, these phrases are getting lost in the communication shuffle. Remember to utilize these phrases when communicating in every form.

When my daughter was two years old, she watched Barney, the show about the purple dinosaur, religiously. In one episode, the kids sang a catchy tune: *"please and thank you they're called the magic words"* (I can *still* hear them singing it in my head). As annoying as it was to hear that song a billion times, there was truth to it. These phrases *are* magic because they show respect and value to the customer. I suggest using these phrases as much as possible in your business, no matter how formal or informal the communication with a customer may be. It is fairly common to begin a relationship with formalities and politeness, and for that to erode with familiarity and our comfort level. This is a mistake. Always be polite with every customer every time you communicate with them. They should always feel like a rock star.

Be very cognizant of using these phrases in all your forms of communications, including face-to-face, phone, email and text. It's fairly natural to be polite with someone in person. The one area of communication that manners and politeness seem to get lost entirely is with texting. More businesses use texting as a simple and effective way to communicate with customers. Business communication via text can be short, sweet, and to the point. It's cheaper and less time-consuming than making phone calls. The problem is texting seems to get more and more informal. I'm looking at my phone right now at a reminder text. It starts with a *hi*. There's no please, thank you, or you're welcome. I'm not necessarily offended by this, but I definitely don't feel valued or important. If Power Phrases were as common as abbreviations and emojis it would help to set a business apart from their competition.

The phrase "my pleasure" is prevalent with many businesses. This is my personal pet peeve regarding manners. There are better phrases to communicate respect. Let's say I'm at an upscale restaurant and having a great meal. The server is doing a great job and taking care of all of the details. They refill my iced tea and I say, 'thank you' and they respond with "my pleasure." I'd rather hear 'you're welcome'. If the goal is to make me feel important, why would I care if it's the server's pleasure to do so? As a consumer, I don't care if you get pleasure out of helping me. I'm concerned about getting help and being made to feel valuable for spending my money with your business. When "you're welcome" is used, it communicates that the customer is the focus of the transaction or the service. Saying "my pleasure" communicates more of a focus on the business or employee. I realize I'm splitting hairs here, but hopefully, you can see the difference in the subtlety of who the focus is on with these two phrases. Another phrase commonly used is "no problem." This introduces the idea that it could be a problem to offer service. As a customer I don't really care if it was a problem. Their job is to take care of me.

The little things matter.

Your business already communicates with the customer on an everyday basis. Good manners will add to the element of respect and value that customers crave.

66

Whatever the mind can conceive and believe, it can achieve.

NAPOLEON HILL

CHAPTER 20:
COMMIT TO COMPLIMENTS

Everybody loves to receive a sincere compliment. When a compliment is given at an appropriate time with the correct intent, it can create a tremendous positive impression on the person receiving it. A compliment makes us feel good and gives us an immediate boost in self-esteem. A compliment makes the customer feel important and valued.

In my clinic, we tried to give every patient a compliment regularly. Naturally, some patients accepted compliments more easily than others. It's important to remember that everyone has something good about them. The key is to look for the good and tell it to them. In a time when people are more isolated, many people are starved for attention. When you give them a sincere compliment, it can be powerfully positive for them. Compliments can have an immediate effect in making a customer feel special.

The last thing you want to do is to make a compliment feel weird or awkward for the receiver, so it's important to be careful. You don't want to create a question in the back of their minds and have them wondering if your motive is something other than making them feel good. To make giving compliments more effective, here are the three guidelines to follow:

BE GENUINE

The best compliments come from the heart. Communication happens partially through our words, but also through our body language. When the two don't sync up, it's apparent. For example, when young siblings have an argument and the parents step in and make them say something nice about the other, they'll dutifully comply, but with a scowling face and crossed arms. It makes neither sibling feel better and only ends up being a lesson in obedience. If the person receiving a compliment can sense a compliment is forced, it completely defeats its purpose. Make sure when complimenting that it's genuine, heartfelt and intended to make the receiver feel good. A compliment is better not given if there's not a good intention behind it.

You also want to make sure the compliment is not contrived. You want the compliment to be natural and spontaneous. You can give some forethought to the compliments you'll give, but you don't want to sound like you're saying the same thing to everyone who walks in the door.

DON'T BE CREEPY

Hopefully, this one is fairly obvious to you. Creepy compliments carry a sexual undertone or are given to an inappropriate person or in an inappropriate setting. It's also worth mentioning that the person receiving a compliment can misinterpret your words, making it inappropriate. There are thousands of neutral compliments you can give that steer you clear of anything inappropriate. The rule of thumb is, don't give a compliment that can be taken any way but friendly.

NOT ALL THE TIME

When you try to give a compliment to every customer every time you see them, it can seem contrived and disingenuous. You really need to pick and choose how frequently you give compliments. In my office, we complimented those that we knew were having a tough time or seemed unhappy more often. I had a male patient that was a negative, unhappy and complaining person. I made it a point to compliment him every single time he was in the office. My actual goal was to get him to smile before he left. More times than not, I could get him to crack a smile. The patients that were the most difficult would often become our best patients. They discovered our attitude of service was behind the compliments.

Here's a short list of areas you can consider when giving compliments:

Their attitude	Their vehicle	Always paying on
Their friendliness	Their jewelry	time
Their family or	Their watch	All the referrals
kids	Their clothing	they've sent
The work they do	(appropriately)	Their patience
Their punctuality	Their helpfulness	Their business
		Their support

Giving a compliment takes the focus off of the employee or the business and puts it squarely on the customer. Compliments also help to build trust and likability. Customers do business with those they know, like and trust. Getting to know a business is the easy part. Liking and trusting will take a little more time and effort. Giving sincere and genuine compliments goes a long way toward these efforts. We all like people who make us feel better about ourselves.

Complimenting is a simple and easy way to foster loyalty to your business.

"

As I grow older, I pay less attention to what men say. I just watch what they do.

ANDREW CARNEGIE

CHAPTER 21:
AVOID THE "NO"

Think back to when you were a kid and to a time when you really had to have something. Maybe it was a toy, or some clothing, or shoes, or a video game – whatever it was, you're dead set on getting it. You're excited. You enthusiastically ask your parents if you can get it, and in your kid brain, you're extremely hopeful, even a little certain that they'll say yes.

You're destroyed when you hear "*No. You don't need that.*"

You're compelled to ask *why*.

"*Because I said so.*"

This offers no comfort, no easing of the sting. Your expectations are totally crushed. You're left feeling shot down for no apparent reason other than what seems like a parental whim.

We experienced this as kids, and if you're a parent, you have done this to your children.

This is very similar to how a customer feels when told NO when dealing with a business. Just like a kid, the customer will need and ask for things. Unlike a parent blurting out NO, businesses obviously need to have a different approach.

A business can't fulfill every wish of every customer. That's impossible. Sometimes, NO is the only answer. It is possible, however, to reframe the NO into something more positive, allowing the customer to continue to feel valued and important – and not like we did as kids when our parents shot us down.

A typical response from a business when telling the customer "NO" is:

> *I'm sorry we can't do that.*
> *That's not available.*
> *We won't be able to do that today.*

These responses take out some of the sting of being told NO, but still leave the customer hanging, in a sense. The customer noticed you were somewhat polite about saying NO, but they will still feel short-changed because there's no explanation.

How to tell a customer NO is to let them know what you can do and not what you can't. If that's not a possibility, then use incentive to make things right for the customer.

The employee could respond with *I'm sorry we don't offer that here, but here's what we can do and here's what we do have. Would you like me to go over some of the details?*

Both of these responses are focused on what the business *can* do for the customer to make them happy.

What if you have nothing to offer the customer who wants X product or service? This is where the business can step up and give a discount, coupon or some kind of incentive. The principle to understand is that the business avoids saying NO to the customer. Saying NO to a customer makes them feel unimportant and unvalued. Flipping the script and changing the NO situation into a positive will help the customer feel valued.

These little things are so powerful in creating an exceptional customer service culture. They turn a negative into an opportunity to please the customer. This is powerful psychological information to drive the customer's perception by how you make them feel. When you can turn a NO into a positive or a mistake into a win for the customer, the perception they have is this business does whatever it takes to make me feel special.

A YES attitude must be cultivated in business. YES, we will do whatever it takes to make you happy. Whatever the customer asks or needs, we will do our best to accommodate them. If we can, we will do our best to satisfy their needs with similar products or services. If we can't, we will try to make the situation right by making it up to the customer in some way. The YES attitude is very *proactive*. If the YES attitude is programmed into the business mindset the employees feel empowered to take action to make the customer happy. The YES attitude is not dependent on the weather, the emotions of the employees, the emotions of the customer, the day of the week, or the time of day. The only variable is figuring out what needs to be done to make things right.

Having the YES attitude creates a positive effect on your employees. They can keep their focus on serving without thinking if they can, want, or should do something for customers. They only have to think about what they will do to make a happy customer, and then do it.

Look for the opportunities to change NO to YES in your business. You will be amazed by how effective and easy it is to do.

66

Destiny is no matter of chance. It is a matter of choice. It is not a thing to be waited for, but a thing to be achieved.

WILLIAM JENNINGS BRYAN

CHAPTER 22:
BOOKEND THE EXPERIENCE

Have you ever greatly anticipated seeing a new movie that falls way short of your high hopes for it? Maybe you enjoyed it, but it just wasn't as great as you anticipated or wanted it to be. Or perhaps, there were parts of the movie you enjoyed, but parts you didn't. It's not all that common to think a film is great from start to finish.

Just like a movie, the customer may give your service mixed reviews. A business should strive to excel at being exceptional throughout the customer's *entire* experience. Customers are most likely to remember the exciting beginning and the last moments of their experience with you. Bookending the customer's experience positively and enthusiastically goes a long way. (Now, I'm not saying your service can stink in the middle.)

Successful bookending means a customer's experience starts with an enthusiastic and Overly Friendly greeting because you're excited to serve them. Their experience ends as you send the customer on their way with enthusiasm because you're excited that you could serve them. At the beginning and the end of their experience, you want the customer to know *you care about them* and that they are important to your business.

When the ending is shoddy, it doesn't feel good. If we call to talk to a service provider, and they take care of the problem you called about, but at the close of the call, all they say is goodbye, it doesn't feel good. If we go to a restaurant, experience good service and eat good food, but upon leaving, the host says nothing at the exit, it is kind of a letdown. When checking out at a store and the clerk maybe says hi, but then only hands you the receipt after you've paid without giving a parting farewell, we feel unfinished (like when the movie just suddenly ends). None of these scenarios are devastating. No one is being extremely rude to the customer. But the customer is left with the sense they didn't matter. The focus of exceptional customer service is to always make the customer feel important *throughout* their experience. A bad final impression is often the only impression the customer remembers. Bookending is a fantastic first and a fantastic last impression.

In being Overly Friendly, we looked at greetings. Now let's review parting phrases.

YOUR FAREWELL

You want to acknowledge that the customer is leaving and send them off with an enthusiastic goodbye. Here's some examples of some great parting phrases.

> *Have a wonderful day!*
> *Have a fantastic weekend!*
> *Thank you for coming in today!*
> *Thank you for letting us serve you today!*
> *If it's around a holiday or a special event for your client – tell them to have a great 4th of July, or Mother's Day, or a relaxing vacation!*
> *I/ we appreciate you – have a great day!*

The phrase I said to my patients on almost every visit basis was *I appreciate you.* I wanted them to know that I appreciated their trust in me as their chiropractor and that I didn't take that for granted. Your objective should be to send the customer off feeling great about themselves and excited to do business with you again. This can be done face-to-face, over the phone, and it's just as important through email and text. Communication is communication no matter what form it's in.

SMILING AND EYE CONTACT

As with our greetings, our partings should be Overly Friendly. Smiling and eye contact are attentive gestures.

Your farewell needs to be given the same importance in all forms. Obviously, you can't make eye contact or give a smile physically through the phone, via email or text, but we know a smile can be heard over the phone, and the right parting phrase in text can exude warmth and gratitude.

Bookending the customer experience is similar to a great sermon or speech. A great speaker will draw you in with the opening, which grabs your attention. As they go through the body of their speech, you are focused on the content because they initially grabbed your attention. Then they close with inspiration or a call to action that makes you want to act , or makes you feel something. You may not remember everything that was said, but you remember how it made you feel.

"People will forget what you say, they will forget what you do, but they will never forget how you make them feel." – Maya Angelou

Dr. Angelou gets to the heart of why you want to bookend your customers' experience with Overly Friendly enthusiasm.

66

The starting point of all achievement is desire. Keep this constantly in mind. Weak desire brings weak results, just as a small fire makes a small amount of heat.

NAPOLEON HILL

CHAPTER 23:
GO THE EXTRA MILE

It is impossible to "wow" your customers every single time you interact with them. That expectation is so high and just can't be accomplished day after day, year after year. Businesses burn themselves out very quickly attempting to achieve the impossible. Customers are not looking to be "wowed" every single time they do business with a company. What the customer wants is to have consistent, friendly service every time they interact with a business. This is very possible for a business to do. It's not the grand gestures, but the small actions done consistently that produce the best results. The little things show the customer that you're there to serve. The big actions done once in a while impress the customers just once in a while. Inconsistent "wow-ing" coupled with inconsistent customer service basics won't inspire loyalty. But if the basics are consistent, and you have the opportunity to go the Extra Mile, you'll find the bigger gestures effective.

If I buy flowers for my wife every week (not that she doesn't deserve them) they wouldn't seem particularly special. It would be something nice I did for her, but not really surprising or impactful. If I buy her flowers a few times a year, that makes a more significant impression.

So, what does going the Extra Mile look like for a business? What you don't want it to look like is a single repetitive action like buying flowers for my wife every week! It should feel spontaneous. Your employees will need specific guidance from you about going the Extra Mile.

GIVE THEM SOME FREEDOM

Some businesses are so rigid about employees making independent decisions about doing something good. They're even reprimanded. If that's the case, then no employee will step up for fear of getting in trouble. Your employees should know what's available to them and to your customers when an opportunity to go the Extra Mile presents itself. Owners and managers need to communicate the parameters of service, giving the employees confidence and the tools to make choices about customer appreciation and going the extra mile.

ENCOURAGE YOUR PEOPLE

Praise your employees for a job well done and for going above and beyond. The rule of thumb I followed was, praise and encourage at least twice as much as you criticize. This will reinforce the correct actions and create a tremendous boost to the employee's self-esteem and confidence.

GIVING MORE

One of my favorite restaurants gave my family two free desserts because it took longer than 20 minutes for them to get food to our table after we ordered. Honestly, it felt like a normal amount of time to wait. We didn't know they had this policy. So, when the manager stopped by to apologize and served us the desserts, it felt like they were going the Extra Mile.

In my practice, I would meet a patient after hours or on a weekend when they were in dire need of treatment. This never felt like going the Extra Mile to me, but the perception my patients had told me it was, and they were always very grateful.

Recognizing the need, sensing the opportunity when it arises, and taking the action is Extra Mile service. The Extra Mile is spontaneous. It's a response, and it's a fantastic tool to garner loyalty.

"

I discovered this simple truth - that you have
been designed with greatness for your
success right within your DNA.

ASRA LOVEJOY

CHAPTER 24:
PUT YOURSELF IN YOUR CUSTOMERS' SHOES AND LOOK THROUGH THEIR EYES

For a short time, I developed tunnel vision with my business. I started with a clear concept of what great service should be. That idea morphed a bit over time and I found myself offering mediocre service and only taking care of the customer at my convenience. I never lost focus of serving my patients and trying to be the best part of their day. I got off track with certain policies and procedures. I maintained certain rules only convenient for me and I lost sight of what was best and most convenient for my patients. What opened my eyes and ultimately helped me to change these procedures was to embrace patient complaints. I realized that the patients weren't complaining just to complain! They were voicing their opinions and communicating their perspectives. Once I understood that and started seeing through my patient's eyes, I was able to create an even better experience for them in my clinic.

Business owners often get into the habit of running their business in a certain way on cruise control. This is easy to do because we're creatures of habit. Sometimes the only thing that can snap us out of our habits is a major breakdown in the system.

"Always put yourself in others' shoes. If you feel that it hurts you, it probably hurts the other person, too." – Rachel Grady

To avoid a major breakdown in your business, put yourself in your customers' shoes. Thinking about each customer's experience will help you be more empathetic toward them.

> em·pa·thy
>
> noun
> the ability to understand and share the feelings of another.

In understanding your customer's problems, concerns, and issues, you gain a greater feeling for them. You'll care for them more. If you understand their story and their needs, you'll deepen the relationship between you. With empathy, the business stops seeing customers as numbers and more as people. You'll see what can be changed or improved to make a better experience for them. You'll understand their physical and psychological experience. You'll see how your business impacts them emotionally.

There are several ways to envision your business through your customers' eyes. You can survey the customers to get their general perspective. This will give you insight into what they experience and may want improved or changed. Many customers don't want to be critical, so they hold back if they don't like something. To encourage their honest input, solicit a really trusted and loyal advisor or long-term customer to investigate on your behalf. Give them free rein in their effort to help you improve. If they feel like they are helping the business improve, they won't shy away from criticism. You can also hire a secret shopper to critique the business. An outsider with no preconceived ideas can be objective and offer their unbiased opinion. You can also conduct your own self-assessment as the business owner. Challenge yourself to *actually* put yourself in your customers' shoes and imagine what they go through. If you can be objective in your observation, you'll understand what the customer feels. One of the most effective strategies to learn about your customers' experience is to hire a consultant or coach. Having someone experienced in your corner is an important investment.

Whichever assessment tactic you utilize, it's best to repeat this once or twice a year. Getting in the habit of seeing the business through the customers' eyes will help the business stay focused on always doing what's best for the customer.

When you're working to understand your customers' experience, you might find that you've forgotten WHO they are. If you are selling t-shirts but overlooking the data that your client base is primarily teenagers, you might not be offering the experience and procedures they are accustomed to as consumers. This information is easily discovered when you track the data. When you truly understand who your customer is, you can better imagine what their struggles or problems are. We are a diverse population and it's enormously helpful to identify your people. Maybe your product or service is popular with a certain occupation. Selling cameras and accessories to professional photographers is a whole different ball game than selling the same equipment to folks wanting to look back upon a vacation or a cruise. Knowing who the customer is and what they want will help you understand what might be common struggles for them. You can then become truly empathetic to their struggles, and this empathy helps you to become more accommodating to the customer.

Any and every aspect of the business should be examined. One aspect is the most commonly overlooked. That is the physical look and feel of the business. The details matter! Scuffed paint, cracked tile or weeds in the parking lot will be noticed by your customers. The business owner and employees get used to seeing things and they no longer register. A messy storefront may not be the single cause for a customer to leave, but it puts a question in the customers' mind about how the business will attend to the details. This is the first impression the customer will have, even before encountering an employee. Physical appearance makes an impact.

"

All you need is the plan, the road map, and the courage to press on to your destination.

EARL NIGHTINGALE

CHAPTER 25:
ANTICIPATION

Have you ever been to a business where the employees seem to know exactly what you might buy or what kind of service you might need? It feels like they take care of your needs before you even know you have needs. Top-tier restaurants are usually very good at this. Your water glass is filled before you're thirsty. Bread is on the table as you open your menu. The utensils you need are on the table before the corresponding food is severed. Your last bite is the cue for a cleared platter. These restaurants train their staff to be on top of every detail and to recognize the cues for what the customer might need next. It's not that difficult to train the anticipatory cues into your customer service which create a strong impression for the customer.

Most businesses have core items and actions that occur repeatedly, day in and day out. In my clinics, I examined and adjusted patients every day. The conditions and personalities differed from patient to patient and the treatment varied accordingly, but my methods to diagnose and process were often the same. I could easily predict that customers would react in certain ways and would need certain things. Anticipating these things and having solutions ready helped them to feel confident in my treatment strategies. Here's how to get in front of your customers' needs.

OBSERVE

In the everyday grind of business, it's easy to be focused strictly on the actions of the day. Tunnel vision evolves wherever anything is habitual or routine. Human beings are creatures of habit because we like things to be easy.

Doing actions repeatedly allows us to get smarter. We can make things easier on ourselves. Soon, we're on autopilot. When actions become so habitual, we lose our capacity to be thoughtful.

The purpose of observing is to understand what is actually going on. When we start observing, we notice the cause and effect that occurs.

"You can observe a lot by just watching."

-Yogi Berra

Yogi speaks the truth. There is beneficial information in stepping back to see things from a wider perspective.

NOTICE THE TRENDS

Once you observe, you need to process what is actually happening. In the regular course of everyday business, you'll find patterns. When you play the part of an observer, you'll be able to really see things.

A hotel owner will notice that when customers check-in, their room isn't always ready. Now they create a process that anticipates this possibility. It is policy to upgrade people into a better available room at no extra charge. It's possible to offer free luggage storage. It's also possible to give them vouchers for use at the lounge. With these permitted, anticipated fixes, a customer's perception will be that the business is looking out for them because the inconvenience comes with solutions. The customer doesn't know or care if the anticipation is spontaneous or premeditated. The effect is the same.

In my chiropractic practice, we observed that patients would experience soreness after their first few treatments. Anticipating this would happen, I would tell these patients to expect this to happen and not to worry. I assured them that it's a normal part of the process. This put the patient at ease because they knew what to expect and prevented them from worrying in the future and losing faith in me.

What trends are happening in your business?

BE PREPARED

After discovering a trend, it's time to prepare for these common occurrences. You'll decide what to communicate at this point. You'll figure out what actions to take. You'll be smarter about your customers' needs before they unfold. As your employees also become more aware, they will anticipate things that even you aren't seeing. Training employees to observe and anticipate and then giving them freedom to take action will empower everyone. Listening to your employees, who are your boots on the ground, is just plain smart. Often, they know what to anticipate more than your leadership. Either way, there are opportunities to delight the customer.

It takes a little work and preparation to successfully anticipate your customers' experience, but it is worthwhile to help them see your business is there for them.

66

There are two primary choices in life: to accept conditions as they exist or accept the responsibility for changing them.

DENIS WAITLEY

CHAPTER 26:
STRATEGIES FOR IMPLEMENTING

My wife really likes IKEA. I appreciate that their giant stores are incredibly organized and sparkling clean. Their furniture is affordable and of fairly good quality. My only issue with IKEA is having to put their stuff together. They package everything very well with labels and instructions, but I absolutely dread having to put the furniture together. I mean, it physically hurts my head to think about it. Not because I can't, but because I would rather do a million other things than take the time to decipher which piece of board goes with whichever screw into whatever slot. The last couple of times we've bought from IKEA, I've hired someone to put the items together (judge all you want). I consider it some of the best money I've ever spent! I pay for a great service and it allows me to keep my sanity and my religion.

How will you assess your customer service and make it the absolute best for your business?

Just like I hire someone to assemble my furniture from IKEA, you can hire someone to assess, strategize, develop, train, implement and monitor your Customer Service Culture. I would love to do that for you (you can contact me through my website – drkellyhenry.com). Often, business owners want only to be trained to develop their own systems. They imagine they will train their employees and oversee implementation. That's where the dread comes in. It ends up being more work than you'd think. It does no good to get the information and not move forward with it in practice.

As a chiropractor, I'd learn something at a seminar or conference and be super excited to get back to the office on Monday and apply everything I'd learned! Balancing the implementation of these new ideas with the work and expectations of my employees and customers was tricky business. Eventually, reality and overwhelm set in and my excitement for the new idea wasn't enough to get anything going in a substantial way. Improving customer service is not like buying some new gadget or a piece of equipment. It will change your business. But only if you'll take action and make it happen.

Here are some strategies to get started.

KEEP IT SIMPLE

"Simplicity boils down to two steps: Identify the essential. Eliminate the rest."

- Leo Babauta

I have lived by this philosophy for most of my life. I value simplicity. It makes sense to identify the essential. I try to narrow down the most important aspect of an undertaking and focus on the path of least resistance to bring about the greatest results. I never try to do everything all at once, because it becomes overwhelming to the point of not doing anything.

If you are going it alone with revamping your Customer Service Culture, focus on one action or one idea at a time. I recommend starting with the simplest or easiest item first. It helps to have some initial success, which will build confidence and inspire you to take more action. You want to build positive momentum toward making positive change.

THIS IS A WORK IN PROGRESS

If you've been in business long enough, you know that things are ever-evolving due to many factors. We often get caught up in where we want to go immediately and never stop to look back at how far we've come. It's easy to feel disheartened because we haven't achieved a goal. We forget all of the progress made along the way!

A simple shift in mindset is part of your progress. Putting specific ideas in place is good work. And then remembering that you've *done* these things is part of the evolution toward real change. Your business is either working to get better or it's getting worse. Remember that seeking, imagining, and implementing new strategies takes time and effort. Allow this effort to build.

My wife tells me that I'm a work in progress. I'm always getting better and I'm definitely better than when she married me. Stay persistent. It will pay off over time.

LET IT BE IMPERFECT

"Imperfect action is better than perfect inaction."

- Harry S. Truman

Many wait until everything is exactly right before they take action. Most of the time, things will never be exactly right to get started on something.

"Ready, fire, aim. Do it! Make it happen! Action counts. No one ever sat their way to success."

- Tom Peters

There are certain decisions and actions that require caution because of the long-term consequences. But usually, imperfect action with subsequent course correction will get you further faster.

Action reveals the necessary adjustments. If you wait until things are just exactly right before you act, you'll never start. You won't learn as you go. And, if you launch when you believe everything is perfect, you will still have to correct the course because you can't account for everything. Allow things to be imperfect for a while. Take imperfect action, monitor the outcome, train to improve, take more action, and repeat. It's like surfing. You can't get caught up in waiting for the perfect wave. There's no such thing as perfect. There is only this imperfect wave to experience and to improve. While the upside of implementing and utilizing exceptional customer service is phenomenal and undeniable, ideas of perfection can create resistance to change. Ride this wave. Do it now.

"

The mind, once expanded to the dimensions of larger ideas, never returns to its original size.

OLIVER WENDELL HOLMES

CONCLUSION

Customer service is an asset or a liability for a business. It can either create tremendous growth and profits or contribute to losing customers in droves.

Be encouraged: it's not complicated to improve your level of service.

I've shared simple ideologies and strategies that will create huge results when done consistently. You will have to develop a plan, train, implement, perform and monitor regularly. If not, the best of intentions are forgotten within a few weeks, like a lot of New Year's resolutions. Commitment is needed to develop this new powerful culture in your business.

Always remember there is no downside to improving customer service. The basic premise of exceptional customer service is making the customer feel happy, important, appreciated and special. Who doesn't want to feel like that? Who doesn't want to have their self-esteem boosted?

Very few actions will generate the phenomenal and long-term ROI that exceptional customer service will. You'll be hard-pressed to find another activity, process, or strategy that consistently brings in more customers and retains them than great customer service does. That's why exceptional customer service is called the new advertising because your customers become walking advertisements for your business. Exceptional customer service will eliminate the need for excess marketing, contributing to your bottom-line profits. It's an absolutely beautiful thing when your customers *become* your marketing agents and the mouthpiece for your business.

The very basic purpose of a business is to get a customer, keep a customer, and to make a profit, so it makes perfect sense to invest in the experience your customers will have.

Be the best part of each customer's day. Make sure that your customer leaves feeling better after having interacted with you and your employees. You never know what people are going through and your business can turn a terrible day into a fantastic one. It's important to remember that you're not just influencing that customer. You're potentially influencing all of the people that every customer will go on to meet. If your customer leaves your business smiling, they're likely to pay it forward and put a smile on someone else's face. It just ripples out from where it started. Let it start with you.

Good luck on this journey. I'm here to support you in any way I can. Reach out to me with any questions: kel@drkellyhenry.com

To Your Success!

Dr. Kel
Dr. Kelly Henry

QUICK FAVOR

I'm wondering, did you enjoy this book?

First of all, thank you for reading my book! Before I ask for the favor, I want to repeat my offer to provide you with a free 30-minute discovery call:

https://drkellyhenry.as.me/

And would you take a quick moment to help me out by leaving a review on Amazon?

Reviews are the best way to help others find this book to increase their customer service and bring about tremendous success for their business.

You can go to the link below and write your thoughts. Thank you!

https://tinyurl.com/drkellyhenry

ACKNOWLEDGMENTS

I want to thank my gorgeous wife and the love of my life Cherry for her constant love, support, and belief in me. To my three amazing kids, Britton, Brady, and Karson, who continually bring me joy and make me incredibly proud. God has blessed me beyond what I could have imagined with my family. I love you all more than I can say!

To my parents Paul and LaVila, and my sister Pam for your never-ending faith and confidence in me. Thank you for raising me in a Godly home; I love you.

ABOUT DR. KELLY HENRY

As a sought-after business consultant, coach, and speaker, Dr. Kelly Henry's purpose is to serve and help business owners ignite their passion and enthusiasm for exceptional customer service. He helps them realize their dreams of ultra-business success and offers a straightforward and practical philosophy and systems to attain them.

From years of ongoing business study and 20 years of trial and error in running his successful clinics, Dr. Henry brings an extraordinary breadth of knowledge for all businesses. His goal is to devise a successful mindset and proven procedures to evolve your business and get it to the top.

Before being devoted full-time to consulting and coaching business owners, Dr. Henry thrived in serving his patients and community while building his personal practice into one of the top 5% of clinics in the country. Currently, Dr. Henry resides in Argyle, TX, with his beautiful wife and three fantastic children.

The key to his business success is his perpetual pursuit of exceptional customer service. He practices what he preaches, and as a result, he now speaks on and coaches the same principles that helped him achieve ultra-success and led him to be one of the premier customer service professional.

www.ingramcontent.com/pod-product-compliance
Lightning Source LLC
Chambersburg PA
CBHW050231270326
41914CB00033BA/1867/J